THE BLACK WIDOWS OF LIVERPOOL

The Black Widows
of Liverpool

A chilling account of cold-blooded
murder in Victorian Liverpool

by
ANGELA BRABIN

Books of related interest

Liverpool: A People's History (2008)
Liverpool in the sixteenth century: a small Tudor town (2007)
Georgian Liverpool: A Guide to the city in 1797 (2007)
Murder in Edwardian Merseyside (2009)
Merseyside Murders of the 1920s (2007)

www.carnegiepublishing.com
www.palatinebooks.com

For information about self-publishing see www.scotforthbooks.com

The Black Widows of Liverpool

Copyright © Angela Brabin, 2003, 2009

First published in 2003, second edition 2009
by Palatine Books,
an imprint of Carnegie Publishing Ltd
Carnegie Publishing Ltd
Carnegie House,
Chatsworth Road
Lancaster LA1 4SL

www.carnegiepublishing.com

British Library Cataloguing-in-Publication data
A catalogue record for this book is available from the British Library

ISBN 978–1–874181–60–6

Typeset by Carnegie Book Production, Lancaster
Printed and bound by Cromwell Press Group Ltd

Contents

CHAPTER I

Pandora's box

' ... there is reason to believe that crime of this kind is far from rare.'

Home Office Memorandum

M OST PEOPLE have had the experience of rummaging around in a drawer looking for a pair of socks and finding instead a faded photograph or a long-lost bracelet. Distracted by the unexpected find, the socks are forgotten and the more engaging discovery absorbs the finder's interest.

Such was my experience when researching the story of two sisters convicted in 1884 of the murder of the younger sister's husband. I had intended to examine the way their trial was covered in the local press to see whether the facts were presented accurately or exaggerated. Were they portrayed as normal women or were their images distorted to make them appear inhuman? That was the 'sock' I was searching for. What I found was akin to Pandora's box.

It was revealed that three other people had died while living with the sisters. Details of their deaths were given at the murder trial and the local press coined the phrase 'wholesale poisoning' for use in the daily reports describing the progress of the case. There is no doubt that those four people were murdered by one or both sisters.

As my research into the details of the trial progressed, the more it became clear that there were even more victims. The notes taken by the clerks at the committal proceedings and the coroner's court contained oblique references to further suspicious deaths and the press hinted that others had died at the hands of the sisters. After conviction the press

I

became more blatant in their accusations, as shown in this extract from the *Liverpool Echo* on 18 February 1884:[1]

> F and H had both been twice married. It is shrewdly suspected now that all four men were done to death by the infernal craft which these women practised. Their two second husbands are known to have been poisoned.

In fact only one husband, Thomas Higgins, was proved to have been poisoned. Suspicion hovered over the death of Margaret Higgins' first husband, Joseph Thompson, and Catherine Flanagan's husband, John, but there is no proof, so far, that Catherine had been married before John Flanagan came into her life.

Whether Flanagan was Catherine's first husband, whether she killed him, and whether there was a previous man in her life, cannot presently be ascertained. With proof positive that she did kill, small wonder then that her erstwhile friends pondered on whom else she could have murdered.

Even the Home Office Memorandum relating to the laxity of insurance rules[2] refers to the probability that other people were killed. The conclusion is reached that 'It is certain that the prisoners had committed several other similar murders and there is reason to believe that crime of this kind is far from rare.'

Using the press reports and the transcripts from the inquests, together with the depositions from the committal proceedings, I made a list of names of people whom I felt could well have been murdered; that list lengthened with each fresh document I examined. Then, I examined the file at the Public Record Office which contained correspondence between the Director of Public Prosecutions, Home Office and Treasury Solicitor, and memoranda passing between various government departments concerning the case. It was a veritable goldmine of information. It soon became apparent to me that the documents revealed social and cultural mores previously unexplored by historians.

While examining those papers it became evident that there were indeed six other deaths, referred to in a statement Catherine Flanagan made to her solicitor, and additional to those I had already listed. So as well as the four referred to at the trial, my initial research uncovered seven more and the Public Record Office file presented me with another six. All are included in the chapter on victims.

Another, separate list then emerged of the names of other women whom Catherine said were involved in a scheme of insuring and killing, and it was at this point that I realised that I had stumbled across what was, in essence, a killing syndicate.

The question obviously arises, 'Why did no one realise that people were being poisoned?' The simple answer is that some did, or as Mrs Hoare, the loquacious undertaker, put it, 'There was talk.' But the gossip did not reach the ears of the doctors until too late. Patrick Jennings tried to question the doctor who wrongly diagnosed his daughter's cause of death, and was verbally abused and threatened for his pains. Patrick Higgins did succeed in persuading Dr Whitford that his brother Thomas Higgins had been poisoned, and it was this discussion between the two men at the opposite ends of the social scale that prompted the police investigation into all the other deaths.

In defence of the doctors, however, it must be said that when they were called to see a patient whom they were told had symptoms suggestive of dysentery, there would be no reason for them to suspect that those symptoms had been caused deliberately by poison. In the four cases that were referred to at the trial (Thomas and Mary Higgins, John Flanagan and Maggie Jennings) each doctor certified that death resulted from the symptoms which he saw and treated the patient for. The doctors would not have expected the carers to lie about the symptoms, nor would they have expected them to feign grief over a much-loved 'daughter', as Catherine Flanagan did over her lodger Maggie Jennings. The doctors would not have dreamt that their presence was merely being requested to legitimise the poisoning; that they were being duped and manipulated so that they would later sign a death certificate without question. Class and status inevitably enters into this. Would a doctor expect an illiterate Irish slum dweller to be able to deceive him, to anticipate the questions he would ask and provide the answers he expected? In short, would a doctor ever dream he could be outwitted by the likes of Catherine Flanagan and Margaret Higgins? Of course not; and therein lies the failure of the system.

The women at the centre of the research, Catherine Flanagan and Margaret Higgins, were sisters, the daughters of an Irish labourer, William Clifford. Little is known of their early life other than the fact that they were born in Ireland, Catherine in about 1829 and Margaret about 1843. It is unlikely that their arrival in the world caused more than passing comment among friends and relatives, and even more unlikely that anyone would have predicted that their deaths would be announced in a national newspaper. Yet on 4 March 1884 *The Times*[3] devoted thirty-two lines to their deaths under the sombre headline 'Double Execution at Liverpool' and that day's Liverpool *Daily Post*[4] spared its readers no details of the grisly scene at the gaol.

Margaret Higgins and Catherine Flanagan were hanged at Kirkdale Gaol in Liverpool in 1884. They were executed for the murder of Thomas Higgins, Margaret's husband, whose life expectancy decreased in direct proportion to the amount by which his life insurances increased. He was poisoned by arsenic, obtained by soaking flypapers in water, and by the time he died, his life was insured for a theoretical total of £108 4s. 0d.

It was clear that both sisters were involved in the killing and rightly convicted. However, Thomas' death marked the point at which their own downfall commenced and from that day onwards, until their execution, their names were rarely absent from the local Liverpool newspapers. But Thomas was not their only victim.

Catherine was the elder sister and appears in the 1881 census for Liverpool living in Blenheim Street. This was part of the area to the north of the city, a close-knit slum community inhabited mostly by Irish Catholics. She and her family and lodgers had moved from street to street over the years. Various addresses were quoted on insurance forms and given in evidence by witnesses during the course of coroner's inquests and committal statements, but they were all within that relatively small area shown on the map of north Liverpool.

During the inquests and criminal proceedings which followed the discovery of the murders, it became clear that Catherine Flanagan had lived in Liverpool for upwards of twenty years, some of the witnesses recalling her when she was younger. It has not been possible to discover when she came from Ireland nor from which part. One important witness to the death of Thomas Higgins, Mrs Catherine Manville, said in evidence that as a child, some fourteen years earlier, she knew Mrs Flanagan who then lived in the same street, Blenheim Street, and kept a 'Jerry shop'. Thereafter she apparently knew little of her movements or lifestyle. The 1881 census[5] describes Catherine as a licensed broker, a widow and head of the household living at 142 Blenheim Street, Liverpool. It wrongly gives her age as 40, she would have been about 52.

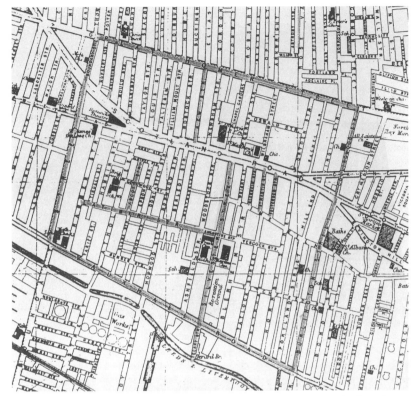

Map of part of Liverpool showing the proximity of people involved in the
murder and their victims.

With her lived her son Patrick (aged 19, labourer, born Liverpool)
and daughter Ellen (aged 10, scholar, born Liverpool); Patrick Jennings
(aged 45, widower, born Ireland) and his daughter Margaret (aged 15,
domestic servant, born Liverpool). There was also another male lodger
called Peter Flanagan (aged 35, labourer, born Liverpool) but apparently
not related, a second lodger, Henry Rimmer (aged 18, labourer, born
Liverpool), and the widowed Margaret Thompson (called May, aged
wrongly 48, she was then about 38, born Ireland, domestic servant),
who was Catherine Flanagan's sister.

Catherine Flanagan was, by that year, a widow, by choice rather than
accident, or so rumour had it. Her husband, John Flanagan, died on 24
June 1879 at 22 St Martin Street. He was a labourer, aged 42. Catherine
was at her husband's side at death, according to the certificate, and
Dr R O'Leary certified his death as being due to 'Pleuro pneumonia,

Blenheim Street in 1971.

fourteen days'. It is quite possible he did indeed die of pneumonia on midsummer's day, but with the benefit of hindsight and knowing that proven victims were similarly and erroneously diagnosed, as will be discussed in the chapter on the victims, doubt lingers.

Throughout the proceedings Catherine was presented as the more dominant of the two sisters, a fact which she denied in her statement to her solicitor (see Chapter 7). She claimed to have been merely the instrument of her sister and other women, taking no part in the killings, merely dealing with the insurance aspect of the deaths. In view of all the evidence this seems unlikely. Nevertheless it is clear that although Catherine and her sister may have been in the forefront of the conspiracy to insure and kill, there were other women heavily involved: this was in effect, a syndicate of like-minded women who also provided shelter when Catherine sought to escape arrest.

Poverty was, then as now, relative. With a reputation as a moneylender, Catherine's income was sufficiently above subsistence level to allow her to wear a silk dress and sport gold rings and earrings. She was illiterate, but this did not prevent her from perpetrating seriously profitable insurance frauds and manipulating doctors and insurance agents to assist her in her poisonous activities. A photograph of Catherine appeared in a memoir written by the Head Constable of Liverpool, William Nott-Bower;[6] sister Margaret is shown in the next photograph from the same source (see above) – at first glance, but only at first, she seems to have a kindlier face, with a clear family resemblance to Catherine.

Certainly Catherine's sister, Margaret Higgins, engineered her own widowhood, for it was Thomas, her husband of only eleven months, whom the sisters were convicted of poisoning. Before Thomas Higgins came into her life, she had been a Mrs Thompson. Joseph Thompson had left her a widow, and a rumour went round that he had shared the same fate as Thomas Higgins. Despite exhaustive searches no trace has been found of Mr Thompson's death.

How long sister Margaret had been in Liverpool is not clear. Witnesses do not seem to have known her as long as her sister; indeed she seems to have been a stranger to many of them. She first appears in the 1881 census living with her sister as a lodger, her occupation a charwoman.

MRS. FLANAGAN.   MRS. HIGGINS.

ON THE CHARGE OF "CAUSING THE DEATH OF THOMAS HIGGINS BY POISON," THESE TWO WOMEN WERE SENTENCED TO DEATH AT THE LIVERPOOL ASSIZES, FEBRUARY, 1884. EXECUTED AT KIRKDALE GAOL, 3RD MARCH, 1884.

Photographs of the sisters from Nott-Bower's memoir.

A waxwork of Margaret Higgins. Models of both sisters were exhibited for many years at the museum of Madame Tussaud.

Her age is wrong, as is Catherine's. She tends to be constantly in her sister's shadow, the follower rather than the leader, described in reports of the trial almost as an afterthought.

Yet Catherine blamed her for the poisonings, offering to give evidence against her in an effort to gain clemency. Her statement, made to her solicitor, put the blame full square on her sister. Who was to blame? Was one sister the leader and the other the follower or were they both tainted with an equal amount of guilt?

As to friends, relatives and neighbours who survived the attentions of the two sisters, they fall into two catagories. The first group were those

who were conspicuous by their absence at the trial, the other women
to whom accusing fingers pointed, like Mrs Evans and Mrs Stanton.
The second group comprised Catherine's friends who had sheltered
her while in hiding from the police, friends whose main concern, once
Catherine was beyond their help, was to keep themselves out of trouble.
Ellen Flanagan, Catherine's 14-year-old daughter, called as a prosecution
witness, stoutly resisted all attempts by the prosecution counsel to
incriminate her mother. Apart from that one ally, Margaret and Catherine
had no friends at court other than their counsel who, in the words of
the press,[7] bravely continued his 'uphill battle' to defend them. Only one
further friend gave them support, Father Bonte, the Catholic Chaplain
at Kirkdale Gaol on the eve and morning of their execution.

I cannot say whether the two sisters were the ringleaders of the
poisoning ring or whether they were merely members under the
leadership of another. Certainly Catherine Flanagan was portrayed as
the most active member, her sister being relegated to the shadows by
her overbearing personality and her behaviour prior to arrest.

Without the benefit of time travel it is impossible to decide which
women were on the periphery of the poisoning syndicate and which at its
centre. Of course the other women (such as Mrs Evans and Mrs Begley)
were never questioned by the police and did not appear as witnesses
for the prosecution. Mrs Stanton was arrested but released after a brief
interval. There are warnings in the Home Office memoranda contained
in the Public Record Office file that certain women would abscond
should police enquiries come too close.

In considering how much weight to attach to the evidence and other
material (some of the information could more rightly be called rumour
rather than evidence), particularly when considering the culpability of
others, I reverted to the disciplines of my profession as a lawyer. I have
tried to reach an objective conclusion as to who was killed, how, when,
and by whom.

As I read through the court documents I realised how little things
had changed over the years. The statements were taken down in a form
still used today. Apart from the unlined paper, the witnesses' statements
would not look out of place in a court file of today. The clerk would write
in longhand a sentence combining the question from the examining
advocate plus the answer from the witness. For example, the advocate
might ask, 'Where did you go after you left home?' and receive the reply

'To see my friend'. The clerk would write 'When I left home I went to see my friend.'

The clerk may therefore superimpose a coherency which may well be lacking from the witness's own phraseology, expanding monosyllabic comments into articulate sentences. It must not be assumed from the witness statements in this case that those witnesses who gave evidence were necessarily as fluent in their answers as the depositions suggest. All emotion is erased; the sheer terror, which envelops some witnesses, cannot be translated onto paper. A witness may think long and hard before committing himself to a definitive 'yes' or 'no', yet hesitations are rarely communicated by the clerk's pen. Only deliberate refusals to answer can be noted. This is not to criticise the clerk; the aim is to put into writing the statement of the witness. Experienced clerks all have their own techniques, interrupting the advocate's questioning if necessary to clarify a point so as to be as accurate as possible. I have no reason to suppose the clerks of 1883 were less diligent than they are today.

MURDER IN VICTORIAN LIVERPOOL

Looking at the statistics quoted in the Liverpool Head Constable's reports for 1883 and 1884,[8] one surprising factor is the low number of murders reported. There is perhaps an expectation that a busy port would naturally attract an element of drunkenness and fighting that could well result in fatal injuries being inflicted. Drunkenness was certainly a problem and detailed figures were kept, breaking down the number of arrests for drunkenness month by month, giving average numbers of arrests for each day of the week, and even for specific periods during the day and night. Hardly surprisingly, the busiest periods for the bobbies in the year ending 29 September 1883 was Saturday between 11 p.m. and midnight, with a total of 923 men and 648 women being apprehended on average for that hour on Saturdays throughout the twelve month period. This was also the peak time for the rest of the week as well, with the quietest moments being between 6 and 9 a.m.[9] The statistics carefully listed the occupations and sex of those arrested for drink-related crimes. In 1884[10] those arrested for being drunk and disorderly included 706 sailors, 1,113 prostitutes, 4 umbrella makers, 38 butchers, 4,267 labourers, 8 surgeons and 2 attorneys. Details were recorded of the age, sex and country of origin of all offenders along with their standard of education, ranging in four categories as 'read and write well', 'read and write imperfectly', 'read' and 'neither read nor write'. The tables in the reports provide a wealth of detail for the social historian. For example, for the offence of 'Threatening by letter with a view to extort money' there was one offender, over 21, male, from Liverpool, who could read and write imperfectly. Another male, aged between 18 and 21 also from Liverpool, was charged with 'Larceny by servant in the Post Office'. He could read and write well.

Taking averages, the trend is the same for all types of offences. The majority (55%) could read and write imperfectly, followed by those who could neither read nor write (33%), then those who could only read (8%), and finally those better-educated people who could read and write well (4%). (These figures were for the period ended 29 September 1883 and the same trend was apparent in the following year's report.) As the Head Constable lamented in his report for 1883, 'no improvement is apparent in the education of the criminal classes.'[11] One assumes he would have been happier if all criminals could read and write well.

However, it is the figures for murder which are more relevant to this story.

Looking first at the Liverpool Head Constable's report for the year ended 29 September 1883, Table 1 shows the number of indictable crimes committed during the twelve months covered by that report. There was one murder of a person over one year old and one male was committed for trial for that offence. There were two murders of infants under one year old (babies under one year were dealt with as a separate statistic in this table) but no one was apprehended for their deaths. There were two attempted murders, both successfully investigated, and thirteen arrests for thirteen cases of manslaughter. Table 31 in the same year's report contains details of inquests for the same period, when the jury in three instances returned verdicts of murder. Thus the two tables balance.

The murders committed by Flanagan and Higgins did not feature in this report, as at the time of printing Thomas Higgins was still alive (although already succumbing to the deadly attentions of his wife and sister-in-law) and thus the other, previous murders had not been discovered and investigated.

In the report for the following year, covering the period up to 29

September 1884, which includes the period in which Catherine Flanagan and Margaret Higgins were arrested tried and hanged, the murder rate rocketed.

In the report for the year ending September 1884, Table 1 notes that seven murders were committed (victims over twelve months old) and this figure would include the murder of Thomas Higgins who died in October 1883. In all, twelve culprits were apprehended for those murders, ten men and our two women.

Table 3 in the same report further sets out the results of the arrests and it seems that three of those men were acquitted, two were still awaiting trial as at 29 September 1884, and five men along with our two women were hanged. There is a surplus of perpetrators over bodies but no doubt, as in the case of the sisters, one or more of the other murders was a joint enterprise.

Turning now to Table 31 which sets out the results of inquests held during the report period, it can be seen that in ten inquests the jury returned a verdict of murder. Taking the original seven murders *committed* during the twelve months to 29 September 1884 (which would include Thomas Higgins) and adding the inquests into the deaths of Maggie Jennings, Mary Higgins and John Flanagan (murders committed *prior* to the period but inquests into their deaths held *during* the period), once again the figures of murders and inquests balance. One assumes that those additional deaths, being discovered so long after the murders occurred, were not likely to have been included in any of the official statistics; it was hardly possible to add them retrospectively.

The Head Constable wrote: 'I regret having to report that during the year the crimes of murder have been unusually numerous and atrocious.' He does not amplify his remarks. Yet he could have congratulated his men on bringing the 'Wholesale Poisoning Case' to a satisfactory conclusion, and the following year, had he but known, he would be breathing a sigh of relief when he would see that the murder figure was back down again to just one (Table 1, 1885). The year after that, ending for the purposes of his report on 29 September 1886, stability would continue with just one adult and one baby being murdered.

Why were there not more murders in this busy port, where drunkenness caused the Head Constable such concern?

It is only when the coroner's inquests are counted that light begins to dawn. There were 729 inquests held by Liverpool City Coroner for the twelve months covered by the September 1884 report. In addition, as the Head Constable says, 'there have been 855 other cases of death reported by the police and others at the coroners court in which, after enquiry by the Coroner, inquests were not been considered necessary.' Thus the grand total of deaths rose to 1,584.

The statistics are quite detailed, dividing the deceased into several categories. Infants were subdivided into legitimate and illegitimate, male and female, under twelve months and between one and seven years old. Thereafter the deceased were graded by age and sex: between seven and sixteen years; between sixteen and sixty; over sixty; and a final 'age unknown'.

Of the 765 inquests held, the jury returned verdicts as follows: ten murders, seven manslaughters, thirty-eight suicides, four hundred and two accidental deaths, forty-seven 'injuries, cause unknown,' and simply 'found dead', a further fifty-seven. In addition under the heading 'Natural Death' (a misnomer if ever there was one) seventy-three deaths were found to have been caused by 'excessive drinking'; three 'disease aggravated by neglect'; four 'want, cold and exposure'; and the ambiguous 'other causes' were responsible for eighty-eight deaths. The figures shown in the 1884 report show trends similar to those of the previous year with the exception of the inflated murder figure.

The answer to the original question 'Why so few murders?' may be a simple one. If a body is found in a dark alley, perhaps without identification, it is surely much simpler and cheaper to decide that he must have fallen and so sustained fatal injuries, than to mount a police murder hunt. A foreign sailor, found on the dock after a fight, with no relatives demanding justice for his apparent unlawful killing, might well be counted as one more statistic for the 'injuries, cause unknown' column.

So, with what appeared to be a much-loved 'daughter' being cared for and fussed over by a distraught and loving 'mother' and exhibiting signs of an illness inherent in the overcrowded slums, what doctor in reality would have wasted time delving into the causes of the illness? Would he not, with alacrity, accept the obvious?

In the case of the 'scam' perpetrated by the two sisters and others, once the death certificate was completed by the doctor and handed over to the grieving relative, funeral arrangements could be made and the insurance money could be claimed. After the interment the profits could then be shared among the investors, and the women, satisfied with the return on their investments, could turn their thoughts to choosing their next victim.

CHAPTER 2

Victims

'*How many people lying in the burial grounds of this and other large towns are there who, if their lives had not been insured, might still be alive at this moment?*'

Mr Justice Butt, in his summing up to the jury[1]

THE DOCUMENTS I HAVE READ show that the hand that proffered a crust of bread to the hungry child could just as easily offer a penny a week to the burial club agent in exchange for a life policy on that same child. The hungry cries of the child could be silenced by a few spoonfuls of liquid obtained by soaking flypapers in water. Tears shed in grief at its death could be blinked away if a profit was made from the club money.

To make it easier to consider the deaths of those people who could possibly have been poisoned by the Liverpool syndicate I have divided the deceased into three groups.

First, those four victims whose deaths were mentioned at the trial: Thomas Higgins who died on 2 October 1883 aged 36; Mary Higgins who died on 29 November 1882 aged 10; Margaret (or Maggie) Jennings who died on 25 January 1883 aged 18; and John Flanagan who died on 7 December 1880 aged 22.

Second, an additional six, all of which were investigated by the police (Catherine Neillan, Catherine O'Brien, 'Mule' [Charles Emmanuel Mure], Mary Donnelly, Mary Flanagan and Emma Godfrey) who were mentioned in the statement Catherine Flanagan made to her solicitor before her trial[2] and discussed at length in correspondence between, amongst others, the Home Secretary, Liverpool's Prosecuting

Solicitor, the Director of Public Prosecutions and the Treasury Solicitor.

The third group comprises seven more deaths that gave rise to local gossip – Michael Flanagan, Joseph Thompson, Stephen Flanagan, John Flanagan senior, Mrs Bridget Jennings, the first Mrs Higgins and Catherine Flanagan's first husband.

There is no doubt that the sisters and their friends poisoned many people for life insurance. There is no doubt about the first group of four, little about the second group of six but considerable dubiety about the final seven.

GROUP ONE

The first group of four victims is obviously the best documented from three sources, namely the notes taken at the coroner's inquests, depositions taken at the committal proceedings and press reports describing all those hearings, plus the trial at the Assize. Unfortunately the judge's own notes are missing but there still exists the letter from Mr Justice Butt forwarding them to Sir A. J. O'Liddell at the Home Office, who had requested sight of them.[3] The mere fact that they were requested gives some idea of the importance this trial assumed at a very high level. It was a long way, in all senses, from the slums of Liverpool to the grand offices of Whitehall. The evidence recorded as given on oath carries more weight than the newspapers' own investigations, where journalists were sent around Liverpool scouting for 'witnesses' who were prepared to 'tell their stories'. Nevertheless, it would be naïve to assume that all the evidence given in court in this case was 'the truth, the whole truth and nothing but the truth'. There are indications that some of the witnesses, particularly Thomas Barrett and James MacKenzie, who assisted Flanagan to hide from the police, may well have taken a more casual attitude to the veracity of the facts to protect their own interests.

Thomas Higgins

In starting with the last victim, Thomas Higgins, I am prompted by logic rather than perversity, for it is his death that set in motion the train of events which was to send Catherine Flanagan and Margaret Higgins to the scaffold. Although both women were charged with other murders (both Flanagan and Higgins with those of Maggie Jennings and John Flanagan, and Higgins alone with the murder of Mary Higgins) the prosecution elected to proceed only on the first indictment, that of the murder of Thomas Higgins. It was the practice of the time to deal with each murder as a separate indictment; indeed such practice continued until the middle of the twentieth century. After legal argument the learned judge allowed the prosecution to put forward evidence of three other deaths by way of similar fact.

Thomas Higgins was described (with nose-wrinkling disdain) in a Home Office memorandum as 'an Irish hodman of the lowest class',[4] but the aftermath of his death sent the Treasury Solicitor post-haste to Liverpool to conduct interviews personally and caused the Home Secretary to write frantic memos during which one can virtually see his blood pressure rising.

Memorandum 26 February 1884.
From Sir William Vernon Harcourt to Sir A. J. O'Liddell[5]
Sir A. O'Liddell,
This horrible story must be investigated with the greatest speed and energy and with all the resources at our command, both with reference to the individuals accused, and the system of Life insurances which has originated these wholesale murders.

The letter of Mr Maule shows how absolutely without resources or utility the office of the Director of Public Prosecutions is for the purpose of dealing with serious cases.

I wish this case placed in the hands of the Treasury Solicitor at once, as the Director of Public Prosecutions has not thought fit to do so.

Place the enclosed papers at once in the hands of the Treasury Solicitor: inform him that the S. of S. [Secretary of State] requests him with the assistance of Mr Mark to employ the whole resources of his Office in the investigation of this terrible business without delay.

The S. of S. desires that no pains or expense may be spared in the investigation.

There can be little doubt that the object of Mr Neale in forwarding this statement is to obtain mercy for the prisoner Flanagan in consideration for the revelations she has made.

This of course tends to cast some suspicion upon the hideous story. On the other hand if it should be corroborated upon enquiry, it will be a matter of serious consideration whether her evidence should not be accepted in order to lay bare the whole of this dreadful business and bring the other criminals to justice.

I instruct the Solr. of the Treasury accordingly and represent to him the extreme importance and urgency of the case.

Write to the Attorney General. Send him copies of the enclosed papers, inform him of the directions given to the Solicitor of the Treasury. Say that the S. of S. would desire to consult him on the expediency of respiting the prisoner Flanagan with a view to taking her evidence. It will be a matter deserving further consideration whether something should not be done in the way of legislation with respect to the unchecked sale of poisonous material like flypaper and also to the system of life insurances which seems to have been pursued with impunity. The Attorney General and the Solr. of the Treasury should be supplied if possible with the newspaper reports of the Trial. Request [*illegible*] to see S. of S. on the subject at the House of Commons at his Room at 5 o'clock tomorrow afternoon Wednesday.

There follows another paragraph which has been made illegible by crossing and scrawling out.

Professor Stevenson, from Guy's Hospital, followed the case avidly in the press and, worried about misreporting of the scientific evidence, wrote to *The Lancet*[6] and the Home Secretary.[7] The latter replied 'personally' to him, there being a note to that effect on the top corner of the professor's letter, but no copy of that letter can be discovered.

Some time after April 1881 (the family was not in residence at the time of the 1881 census) Thomas Higgins made the fatal mistake of taking lodgings with Catherine Flanagan.[8] He, his wife and young daughter Mary moved into 31 New Blenheim Street, or as it was more usually called, Blenheim Street. According to the 1881 census the Flanagan household then consisted of Patrick Jennings and his daughter Margaret; Catherine Flanagan and her son Patrick and daughter Ellen; another male lodger called Flanagan but not related; and the widowed Margaret Thompson, Catherine Flanagan's sister and later co-defendant.

A certified copy of the marriage certificate of Thomas Higgins amd Margaret Thompson, 28 October 1882.

After a short while Thomas Higgins' wife died. Despite continued research, her death registration has not been found. Flanagan's sister Margaret, recently widowed, also lodged in the house and on 28 October 1882[9] she and Thomas married. The entire Flanagan household, including the newly married couple, then moved to 5 Skirving Street. By the end of November 1882 Thomas' daughter Mary, aged about ten, had died as well.

After that the household moved yet again, to 105 Latimer Street, where they remained until the end of September 1883.[10] For some reason Thomas and Margaret Higgins then moved to live alone in the cellar of 27 Ascot Street (off Latimer Street) where, after only ten days, Thomas died on 2 October 1883.[11]

Why Thomas allowed himself to succumb to the sisters' murderous intentions is a puzzle. He had seen his daughter and Maggie Jenning die, he had thwarted attempts to increase insurance on his own life, and judging by his brother's suspicions after his death, he may well have passed information to him along the lines that he suspected malpractice. Had he moved to Ascot with his new wife believing his life would be

A typical Liverpool court of the Victorian era, showing the sort of environment in which the women and their victims lived.

safer away from his sister-in-law? Why, when he was taken ill, did he not communicate his suspicions to his doctor, Dr Whitford? Or did he tell that gentleman only to be disbelieved; his fears dismissed as ramblings, a symptom of his dysentery? Such questions can never be answered. The manner of his sudden illness and death is described in detail at both the coroner's inquests and the committal proceedings, being recorded by the clerk in contemporaneous notes. The evidence is virtually the same in both venues. The same evidence is given again at the Assize Court by the same witnesses and faithfully reported in the local daily newspapers.

Neighbour Catherine Manville gave detailed evidence of Thomas' last few days:[12]

Statement of Catherine Manville taken on Oath before the
Liverpool City Coroner, 14 December 1883 at the Inquest
into the death of Thomas Higgins.

Catherine Manville, being sworn says:

I am the wife of Peter Manville a labourer. We live at 25 Ascot Street in Liverpool. I have known the prisoner Flanagan for about 20 years. I never knew the deceased till a Sunday about a week before his death. He was sitting on his steps. I only knew the prisoner Higgins from the Saturday morning when she came to live in the cellar next to us. That is to say that I saw her for the first time the day before I saw the deceased for the first time. I don't remember the day of the month they came to live near me, but it was a Saturday in September. I saw the deceased again on the next Wednesday following the Sunday I have spoken of. I did not see him again until the Monday night previous to his death on the Tuesday morning. On the Monday evening previous to the deceased's death I saw his wife, the prisoner Higgins. I asked her how her husband was. She said, 'He is very bad would you come in and see him.' On the Thursday evening before I was going down Athol Street and I met the prisoner Flanagan and she said 'My sister's husband is very bad'. I asked her what ailed him, she replied 'He is very bad with the diarrhoea'. I said it was a very bad complaint and she should fetch him somebody. She said she had the Dr to him. On the Monday before the deceased's death I went in when his wife asked me as I have said. He was in

bed, he seemed to be in great agony. He was facing the wall and
moaning and scratching the wall with his fingers of both hands.
No one was with him then but Mrs Higgins the prisoner. I did
not wait long, but I returned at 20 minutes past 10 o'clock that
night. The deceased seemed just the same then. He was able to
speak on each occasion. He said nothing but looked at me when
I first saw him, as his wife told him a neighbour had come in to
see him. When I went in the second time to see the deceased, I
found the wife there and Mrs Flanagan and her daughter Ellen.
When I went in this time nothing was said about the deceased's
ailment. The deceased put his hand on his breast and said 'Oh if
this pain had gone from me' he appeared to me to be very bad
and suffering much. He was working all the time with his hands
as before. I stopped with him going backwards and forwards till
about 20 minutes to 1 o'clock in the morning. I took Mrs Lawton
(a witness) into the deceased's house with me. She lived in the
house above the cellar. At about 12 o'clock on the night I am
talking about I heard the prisoner Flanagan say to the prisoner
Higgins 'Margaret you had better get up and go home you are
tired and you had better go too Nelly' meaning the child. When
Flanagan said this Margaret Higgins and the girl left, leaving Mrs
Flanagan myself and Mrs Lawton in the house with the ailing
man, now dead. Mrs Flanagan then lived in Latimer Street. After
Mrs Higgins had gone I heard the deceased ask for a drink of
water. Flanagan got up and took a mug off the table and took
a table spoon and put it in the mug and was going to give it to
him to drink. She offered him the spoon but he turned his head
away and said 'Take it away, take it away'. She then turned what
was in the spoon back again into the mug and put the spoon on
the table and then threw what was in the mug behind the fire.
It was a little white mug with a handle, a little gill mug. I could
not tell if there was much liquid in the mug. She throwed it far
behind the fire. I had not noticed the colour of it at all. In about
half an hour the deceased again asked for a drink. Mrs Flanagan
was asleep at this time, on a stool in the corner. He asked for
a drink of water. I got up and got a cup of cold water from the
water tap. I got the cup from the cupboard. He turned round his
face from the wall and said 'You are not able to lift my head up'.

I lifted his head up and he drank the cup of water. He then said
after drinking the water 'Oh, God bless you' and he turned his
head and died. I don't know what became of the mug after she
(Mrs Flanagan) had left it on the table.

When the deceased died I woke Mrs Flanagan and said 'Oh
get up, he's dead'. I went to lift his head up as he had worked
it off the bolster when she turned round and said 'Sit down and
mind your own business'. She said nothing more and did not
refer to the deceased being dead. Mrs Lawton was present at
this time. Nothing was said by anyone about getting a doctor to
the deceased in the last few hours of his life. The three of us,
Mrs Flanagan, myself and Mrs Lawton sat together till three in
the morning talking. At three I left and went home. The three
of us left together. Mrs Flanagan was the last out and shut the
door. During the time we were talking about the deceased's death
Mrs Flanagan said she had him in a club and would give it to
Mrs Higgins in the morning and let her bury him decent. Mrs
Flanagan said she would go home and would make Mrs Higgins
a cup of tea and make her get up and come back again.

When I offered the deceased the cup of water he took it freely.
He had asked for it and made no signs of not wishing to have
it. The deceased could speak during the two or three hours prior
to his death and spoke of Mrs Flanagan as the landlady. He
only spoke to the extent of asking for a drink and calling Mrs
Flanagan landlady.

At about 11 o'clock on the morning of Tuesday I saw Mrs
Flanagan pinning sheets round the deceased's bed railings. I
looked in and said good morning and no more. I did not see
Mrs Flanagan again till I saw her leave the house when the
funeral was stopped. I saw Mrs Higgins several times after her
husband's death. She said nothing about his death to me. All
she said about Mrs Flanagan was 'Mrs Flanagan is missing, I
suppose she is drinking. She has taken my dress and shawl.'
Mrs Higgins never once referred to what disease or ailment had
carried off the deceased. Mrs Higgins did not continue to stop
in the cellar. I only saw her outside the railings and she never
referred to her husband's funeral being stopped or to the reason
for Mrs Flanagan going away.

[In answer to questions from Mr Marks:]

Mrs Higgins said that Mrs Flanagan had gone away with
her (Mrs Higgins) gown and shawl. She did not say why Mrs
Flanagan had used her gown and shawl instead of her own. She
said where Mrs Flanagan had gone to she did not know. I did
not ask Mrs Higgins why Mrs Flanagan should have done this.
Mrs Higgins gave me no explanation and I did not ask.

[In answer to questions from the Coroner:]

I have said I knew Mrs Flanagan since I was a girl. I do not
know how often she was married I don't know how she lived.
It is 14 years since I lived in the same street. She then lived in
Blenheim Street and kept a 'Jerry shop'. I have not seen much of
her for the last 14 years.

Catherine Manville X her mark.

Sworn before me

C. Aspinall

Coroner of Liverpool.

At the committal prceedings Mrs Manville added that they had lived
in the cellar under a fortnight, Mrs Flanagan and her girl being the
only visitors she saw. When cross-examined by Mr Neale, solicitor for
Flanagan, Mrs Manville refuted the suggestion that the dying man said,
'Take it away there is spirits in that' and denied that Mrs Flanagan said,
'It is only brandy and water'. (Catherine Flanagan in her statement[13]
insisted 'The liquid I threw behind the fire was Brandy and there was
not more than a teaspoonful in the cup.') When cross-examined on this
point Mrs Manville is adamant that when the liquid was thrown on the
back of the fire it did not affect the fire in any way. She described the
mug as a small gill mug. Mrs Lawton adds one small point which Mrs
Manville does not mention,[14] that Margaret Higgins waved her apron
saying that she was 'sending away from the deceased what was on the
wall', and Mrs Lawton took this to mean that he was hallucinating and
his wife trying to humour him.

Mrs Manville says that there was no suggestion that a doctor should
be called to see Higgins in his last hours. Yet Thomas was already
under the care of Dr William Whitford 'whose duty it was to attend to
cases in the humbler class of life when he was sent for.'[15] Dr Whitford
gave evidence[16] that he attended on Thomas in his capacity as District

Medical Officer in the Parish of Liverpool at Mrs Higgins' request. He called at 27 Ascot Street and found Thomas suffering from irritation of the bowels and stomach resulting from bad drink 'as I then thought'. Thomas did smell of drink and told the doctor that he had been drinking for one or two days. No fever was found, his temperature was normal and Dr Whitford said that he spent 'some time' with him. He seemed a strong and vigorous man and although the original note that Mrs Higgins had brought to the doctor (written by the receiving office) had indicated that the problem was fever, no one thereafter made any reference to fever. Dr Whitford said that he would normally remove a fever case to hospital. He prescribed some medicine, which would have to be made up and fetched from the Burlington Street Dispensary. Mrs Higgins seemed to be in charge of Thomas and when the doctor next called on 29 September, she said she had given him the medicine regularly. On that next visit Mrs Flanagan was possibly present, the doctor was not sure, but added that others, unnamed, were also there. Dr Whitford seems to have been surprised how much Thomas had deteriorated since the first visit, being considerably weaker, and this was not consistent with symptoms of 'bad drink'. His diarrhoea was no better and he was, as a normal consequence, thirsty. No fever was present. More of the same medicine was prescribed, castor oil followed by a mixture of bismuth and opium. The doctor stayed about ten minutes and noted that Thomas complained of pains over his bowels. Dr Whitford, having no reason to be suspicious, ordered a change of diet and told Mrs Higgins to report to him the following Monday morning (1 October). This she duly did, telling Dr Whitford that her husband was no better. A visit was arranged for the following day. However, when he arrived at the surgery the next morning he found Mrs Higgins there already with the news of Thomas' death. Dr Whitford, surprised, questioned her about his symptoms and was told that he 'died somewhat suddenly', the purging and vomiting having continued with blood in the stools. Dr Whitford, without going to examine the body of Thomas, certified the cause of death as 'Dysentery, eight days'.[17]

It seems that the three women, Mrs Lawton, Mrs Manville and Catherine Flanagan, remained with Higgins until his death at about three the following morning (2 October 1883) and then they left, Mrs Flanagan being the last to leave and shut the door. The next day, although Mrs Lawton and Mrs Manville both spoke to the two sisters, nothing was said about the death of Thomas. Mrs Higgins, however, did inform Mrs Manville[18] that Mrs Flanagan had gone off with her (Mrs Higgins') dress and shawl and was missing.'I suppose she is drinking,' said Mrs Higgins. Nothing was said to explain why the funeral had been stopped or why Mrs Flanagan was missing.

During the time the three women were sitting with the dying man and mulling over events Mrs Flanagan was asked if Thomas was insured, and she confirmed that she 'had him in a club' and would give the proceeds to Mrs Higgins to pay for his funeral. It is perhaps quite natural to consider whether the means are to hand to pay for a relative's funeral, but it must be remembered that Catherine Flanagan and Margaret Higgins had spent a great deal of time and effort making sure that he was well insured.

Margaret, with Catherine present, started with a modest amount on 10 December 1882, insuring Thomas' life for £15 with the Scottish Legal Insurance.[19] (Bear in mind he had been married less than two months.) Margaret Higgins made the proposal and paid two premiums but after those Mrs Flanagan paid the remainder. This insurance netted only £7 17s. 6d., as Thomas had died before twelve months had elapsed, and thus the proposer was only entitled to half of the benefit. Mr Cartwright, the insurance representative dealing with the claim, told the coroner:[20]

> There is a fair percentage of deaths in half benefit. I am speaking of adults. We go up to £20 without requiring the insured to be examined by a doctor. I find in my experience people enter lives under £20 to get rid of a doctor's examination.

He continued,

> I paid the money to a female who represented herself to me as Margaret Higgins but I know now the woman I paid it to was the prisoner Flanagan.

Apparently she had given quite a performance, 'sobbing and crying and saying she had lost the best husband in the world'. She put her cross to the name 'Margaret Higgins'.[21]

Having received the registrar's certificate of death from Catherine Flanagan[22] Mr Cartwright handed over the cash to her. Next came the insurance from the British Workmen's Association, taken out on 18 December 1882 for twelve guineas.[23] The representative, Mr Williams, says he was collecting at the time and visited the Higgins' at Skirving Street. Mrs Flanagan was present but the suggestion to insure the new couple came from Mr Williams (who of course would receive commission). Both Margaret and Thomas were then insured and it was not long before Mr Williams returned to pay out £12 9s. 6d. on Thomas' death. He commented to both the widow and her sister that Thomas had died suddenly but was not favoured with any response. Thomas did at least know about this policy.

The next policy was with the Prudential Assurance Company, effected on 26 February 1883 for £15 12s. 0d.[24] It seems Flanagan was urged by her friend Mrs Stanton (of whom we shall see more) to 'find him a member or two it will help him'. After some discussion about amounts, the agent Finegan explained that 3d. a week would insure a person up to the age of 35 for £15 12s. 0d. Finegan says Flanagan, whom he did not know, gave him the name of her husband as Thomas Higgins. She also put in one of her lodgers, Patrick Jennings, saying he was her brother. However, there came a snag. Finegan wanted to see both Higgins and Jennings about their insurance. Flanagan procrastinated, asking if it was necessary for her to tell them they were insured as 'they were rather odd', but eventually told him he could see them any evening. When he duly called, he knocked three times but no one came to the door. Eventually a little girl emerged from an entry. Asked why she did not open the door she said she did not live there. On being asked if she knew Higgins and Jennings she pointed to a man standing under a lamppost some way off and said it was Higgins. Finegan then asked the girl if the men were sober and healthy. He was told that Higgins was sober and Jennings a drunkard. Amazingly Mr Finegan went away satisfied, did not bother to speak to the man by the lamppost and duly accepted the proposal for Thomas Higgins. Much criticism fell upon Mr Finegan at the trial over this lax attitude.[25] For some untold reason a policy was not issued for Patrick Jennings. Fate was clearly on his side.

It is interesting to note that once the policy had been approved for Thomas Higgins, approximately one week later, Mr Finegan tried to deliver the document to 'Mrs Higgins' but could not find her. He told the coroner that he heard 'they' had gone to Latimer Street, but his enquiries proved abortive. About a fortnight later he called on Mrs Stanton and asked where Mrs Higgins had gone. She 'made use of some foul expressions and said she did not know, she said "me and her had some words".' He further adds that Mrs Stanton 'found the premiums all the time'.[26] From subsequent events, one is left with the impression that Mrs Stanton seems to have been referring to the 'real' Margaret Higgins, whereas Mr Finegan was in fact looking for Catherine Flanagan, thinking her name was Margaret Higgins.

After Thomas' death it was to Mrs Flanagan (pretending to be Mrs Higgins) that Finegan paid the proceeds of the policy, amounting to £7 11s. 6d. He too remarked on the suddenness of death and consequent distress, but Mrs Flanagan responded, 'Poor fellow, he was ill longer than eight days'. (It could be true to say that he was dying from the moment he married Margaret.) The money was paid, unbeknown to Mr Finegan, at a time when Catherine Flanagan was already on the run from the police, and was handed over at the home of the ubiquitous Mrs Stanton.

Flanagan had made two abortive attempts to collect the money the night before, 3 October, calling at Mr Finegan's home address 43 Salisbury Road, Everton, just under one mile from her own home.[27] At that point she had no reason to believe that the authorities were in any way suspicious of Thomas' demise and so one wonders why the arrangement was made for the cash to be delivered next day at the Stanton household. There seems to be no answer to this question: one may only surmise that deceit or excessive caution entered into the formula.

The proposal form produced at the committal[28] gives details of Thomas' health and antecedents, all apparently fabricated by Mr Finegan. The cross beside the name Thomas Higgins is clearly a forgery, as on Finegan's own admission he never spoke to him! In addition, his age is given as 35, and place of birth as Liverpool, which was wrong.

The Wesleyan and General Assurance Company was then approached and on 22 February 1883 Thomas Higgins was insured for £25. William Bennett, the agent, gave evidence[29] that the two sisters proposed Thomas, the agent filling in the proposal form.[30]

When Bennett asked to see him he was told he could see him any evening. After a few days he called at 5 Skirving Street and spoke to Mr Higgins, who signed the proposal form, and the policy[31] was issued. The details on the proposal form give an age of 35 and a date of birth of 7 June 1848 in County Cork. All health questions were answered to best advantage and the premium noted as 1s. 4d. monthly. When Thomas

eventually signed his mark he had no way of knowing what the form
said unless Bennett went through it with him. We are not told that he
did. In any event a Dr Bowen examined someone, supposedly Thomas,
on behalf of the society on 20 February 1883.[32]

He described him as 'short, strong, grey eyes, well built', and gave
him a clean bill of health. This policy seems to have been dealt with
properly with Thomas Higgins' knowledge and permission.

The next attempt at insurance was made with Pearl Life in March
1883. John Bowles, who knew Thomas Higgins by sight, went to 105
Latimer Street on 22 March 1883 and filled in a proposal form on
Thomas' life at the behest of Mrs Higgins.[33]

He records, 'Mrs Higgins could not write. I told her to make her mark.
She called Ellen Flanagan to write for her and she wrote something. I
had not my glasses with me and did not then see that she had written
"Thomas Higgins" and made a mark instead of "Margaret Higgins".'
Another £40 was added to the value of Thomas' life.

The District Supervisor, Francis Dominic Bowles, had then to formally
see and 'pass' the proposed insured person,[34] and he explained that he
attended at Mrs Flanagan's house, 105 Latimer Street, and asked to see
Thomas Higgins. A woman, not one of the prisoners, who were absent,
introduced a man purporting to be Thomas Higgins to Mr Bowles.
Mr Bowles was apparently satisfied, filled in the relevant forr[35] to say
Higgins was fit and healthy and issued the policy,[36] backdated to 12
March 1883. A medical certificate was issued on 4 April 1883 saying
that Thomas Higgins was first class insurance material.[37]

Exactly whom it was that the doctor saw, if anyone, we shall never
know, but it seems unlikely that it was the real Thomas Higgins.
However, by chance, it was Francis Bowles who went to 27 Ascot Street
on 3 October to get the claim form signed. While Margaret Higgins
was making her mark on the form he happened to glance at the corpse
of Thomas Higgins and realised it was not the same man to whom
he had been introduced. At the committal proceedings, Mr Raffles,
the stipendiary magistrate, commented, 'What a farce this seeing and
passing must be'.[38] Needless to say, the claim was not paid out, Mr
Bowles making an excuse and leaving hurriedly, later marking the
claim form signed by Higgins[39] as being an 'unjust claim'. He similarly
marked the one put in by Flanagan.[40]

The one attempt at insurance that failed was with the Royal Liver

Friendly Society.[41] Their collector, Mr Jones, called at Latimer Street on 2 April 1883. He heard Mrs Flanagan says to Mrs Higgins, 'We'll put Tom in for £50.' Apparently Mrs Higgins made no reply and Thomas was not present. Nevertheless, Mrs Flanagan told Jones to fill in the form and Mrs Higgins answered all the relevant questions, marking her cross by her name on the proposal form under the declaration 'I, Thomas Higgins'.[42]

Flanagan paid the entrance fee of 3s. 6d., but the policy was not issued because Thomas did not fulfil the requirement to be examined by a doctor. Jones pressed the matter from time to time with Mrs Flanagan and after six weeks he made an appointment to see Thomas between 6.30 and 7 p.m. He and the two sisters sat waiting until 9 p.m. for Thomas to turn up. When he than arrived home Jones told him of his errand. He was not best pleased, and said 'To Hell with the clubs you'll get no money for me'. Jones remarks that he was 'quite sober'. Mrs Higgins then went upstairs, and Mrs Flanagan remained downstairs. Mr Jones wisely did not press the matter and adds rather wistfully, 'Nothing was ever said by either of the two women as to why the man would not go to a doctor.'

Despite this failure, Thomas Higgins' life by this time was insured for a theoretical total of £108 4s. 0d. This would have been a great deal of money as a labourer such as Thomas would expect to earn about 15s. per week.

When he died on 2 October 1883[43] Thomas Higgins was a strong, healthy, 36-year-old man employed as a hod carrier, and had the nickname 'Crack of the Whip' because of his vigour.[44] His brother, Patrick, 'who, although a man in a very humble station of life, appeared to be sensible'[45] (as the Prosecuting Solicitor for Liverpool, Mr Marks, explained condescendingly in his opening speech at the committal proceedings), was an Irish shoemaker aged about 44, who lived nearby at 97 Bannastre Street with his family.[46] It was his uneasy suspicions about Thomas' demise that tolled the death knell for Catherine Flanagan and Margaret Higgins.[47]

Sometime during Tuesday 2 October Patrick Higgins was told by an acquaintance that his brother had just died. He had been on good terms with his brother and was surprised that he had not been warned that his brother was ill or dying. Patrick knew his brother's wife Margaret and her sister Flanagan. He told the coroner at the inquest that Margaret

Higgins 'was as far as I know the wife' of his brother but adds 'I was not present at their marriage'.[48] At the committal proceedings he told the court that 'Something was told me that aroused my suspicions'[49] and he set about making enquiries at all the burial clubs and insurance societies that he knew in the city. Having ascertained that his brother had been insured in many insurance societies, and the amount of club money which was due to be paid on his death, Patrick made his way to the office of the Registrar of Deaths and found the name of the doctor who had attended Thomas in his last illness, Dr Whitford.[50] On the evening of 3 October Patrick went to see Dr Whitford at his home at 37 Shaw Street.[51] The doctor listened to Patrick's suspicions concerning Thomas' death, and advised him to speak to the coroner. This he did and 'at the coroner's request I went and brought Dr Whitford to the coroner at once the same day.'[52] (In fact this would be 4 October.) Together then, Dr Whitford, Patrick and the coroner's beadle* went to 27 Ascot Street where the body of Thomas lay. Margaret Higgins remained in the house but Catherine Flanagan left abruptly, not to be seen again for another ten days. While the coroner's deputation was in the house the funeral coaches came to the door, but the beadle put a stop to the proceedings and Dr Whitford conducted a post-mortem examination of the body then and there. His suspicions, already aroused by Patrick, were intensified by his examination of the body and confirmed when chemical analysis had been made of the various parts of the intestines. Thomas' body was that of a strong healthy man with no signs of disease.

Thomas had been poisoned by arsenic; that, and not dysentery, was the cause of his death. It was at this point that the sisters' scheme began to unravel.

---

*   The coroner's beadle was John Hargreaves, formerly a Chief Inspector in the Liverpool Police force, he was made beadle of the Coroner's Court in December 1881. He died on 26 April 1889 aged 48 and at his inquest, the coroner, Mr Clarke Aspinall paid tribute to him both personally and professionally and expressed his deep sympathy for his widow and seven children. (Report of the inquest in the *Liverpool Mercury* 27 April 1889 and correspondence with Mrs A.Pentecost, great-granddaughter.)

Mary Higgins

Thomas' daughter Mary Higgins did not live long once her father remarried on 28 October 1882.[53] On 9 October 1882 her new stepmother had taken out a policy of insurance on her life for the sum of £22 10s. 0d. with the British Workmen's Association. The child lived for less than seven weeks after that, dying at 5 Skirving Street on 29 November 1882. Her coffin plate records her age as 10.[54] Patrick Jennings, father of Maggie and fellow lodger, recalls the child dying. He said she was ill for six or seven days and died in the room occupied by her father and new stepmother.' Every time I went into the room I found the chamber pot in the bed with her. I heard her vomiting two or three times.'[55] Her uncle – Patrick Higgins – told the coroner[56] that he was not told of her death until after her interment, then his brother came to tell him.

She was buried at Ford Cemetery in an unmarked grave[57] on 1 December 1882. The following day Margaret Higgins collected the insurance settlement of £21 18s. 6d. (11s. 6d. had been deducted as only 1s. 6d. in premiums had been paid[58]). Her body was exhumed[59] on 16 January 1884. In due course her body was laid back to rest in the same grave.

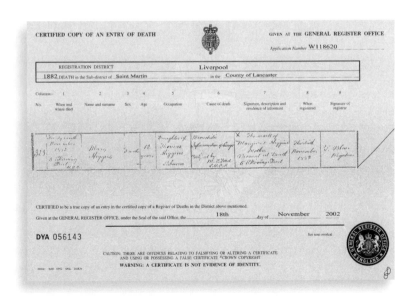

A copy of Mary Higgins' death certificate.

When Dr Frederick Lowndes (Surgeon of Liverpool City Police)[60] examined her exhumed body he noted the colour of her hair and 'a peculiar prominence of the front teeth and a peculiarity of the great toe of the right foot', all of which details he had been given by the two witnesses (the two Patrick Higgins, father and son, her uncle and cousin) who had given descriptions to identify the body. She was 'fairly nourished but not fat'. From her lungs he deduced she had been suffering from 'an acute disease of the lungs, probably pleuro pneumonia', but was otherwise healthy. He was of 'a very strong opinion' that the cause of death was not pleuro pneumonia. (Dr Ford had certified her death as due to 'Bronchitis, Inflammation of lungs'.) From the remarkable state of preservation of the body, plus patches of staining in the stomach and bowels, he concluded that 'an irritant poison, most probably arsenic, had been administered to or taken by the child within a very short period of her death.'[61]

Dr William Whitford, who had attended Thomas Higgins, performed the post-mortem examination with Dr Lowndes and came to the same conclusions.[62] Chemical analysis by chemist Edward Davies found 'considerable quantities of arsenic' present in internal organs.[63]

Catherine Flanagan vehemently denied any knowledge or involvement in this murder in the statement she made to her solicitor before her conviction.[64] She said: 'Mary Higgins was not insured by me at all and I positively assert that I had no knowledge whatsoever that poison had been given to her until my sister told me of it after her death. She was very ill and I thought she died naturally.' Although Catherine Flanagan was originally charged with Mary's murder, only Margaret Higgins was committed for trial. The committal took place at Liverpool City Police Courts in Dale Street on 1 February 1884, and the examining magistrate, Mr Thomas Raffles, endorsed the papers: 'After hearing all the evidence I did not commit the prisoner Flanagan on this charge.'[65]

I am inclined to accept that Flanagan was not responsible for this death, and the responsibility was that of Higgins alone.

Maggie Jennings

The next death was that of 18-year-old Margaret (Maggie) Jennings[66] on 25 January 1883. She and her father Patrick had lodged with Mrs Flanagan for at least ten years[67] in various houses, before moving to 5 Skirving

Street where she died. She is listed in the 1881 census as being 15 years old, a domestic servant and born in Liverpool.

Her father described her last illness in his evidence.[68] He described her as a strong healthy girl, who, with the exception of one illness two years earlier, had always been well. Soon after dinner on 14 January 1883 'she took to vomiting and had to go to bed. She slept in the same room as Mrs Flanagan and her daughter.' This would be Ellen, then aged 13. Margaret Higgins was also living there but Patrick Jennings says she slept in another room, although she helped Catherine Flanagan look after Maggie. Apparently Patrick was out of work the week his daughter died and thus was able to see his daughter 'a good many times between the Sunday and the day she died but I did not see her every day *as I was prevented by Mrs Flanagan*' (my emphasis). He says that he heard her vomiting 'many times *and what she vomited was taken away at once by one or the other of the prisoners*' (again my emphasis). This statement only becomes significant when contrasted with the evidence of Dr Rafter,[69] who attended Maggie on six occasions.[70] He could not get anything direct from the girl as to her complaint; Mrs Flanagan was attending to her and referred to Maggie as her daughter. Patrick Jennings was surprised to hear the doctor call Mrs Flanagan 'Mrs Jennings' on one occasion and he queried this, saying 'By God, you have got a strange name unknown to me,' but Mrs Flanagan merely laughed.[71]

Dr Rafter seems to have been rather nonplussed about the symptoms; he prescribed some medicine and asked to be kept informed of her progress. He duly was and on the second occasion Maggie complained of great pain and a bad cough, whereupon Mrs Flanagan, still assumed by Dr Rafter to be the girl's mother, produced some expectoration containing blood. This prompted Dr Rafter to diagnose pneumonia and prescribe accordingly. A summons two days later found improvement, two days after that a relapse. The final visit on 24 January found Maggie still weaker. Dr Rafter specifically notes that he had every confidence in Mrs Flanagan as 'she appeared very anxious about the girl'.[72] The next day, 'Mrs Flanagan came crying and told me the girl was dead. She called her her daughter.' He certified the cause of death as pneumonia and notes: 'I was not at any time told that she had been suffering from purging or vomiting. When I asked about her bowels Prisoner Flanagan said she was quite regular.' Dr Rafter stated that he did not administer arsenic to the girl in any form. This comment was no doubt prompted by a direct question from the prosecution to anticipate and negate any defence suggestion that the arsenic may have been an ingredient in the prescribed medicine.

It is hard to find any innocent reason why a doctor would be called on so many occasions yet given misleading information about symptoms. The conclusion must be that the motive was to allay any suspicions of malpractice and thus obtain a death certificate without awkward questions being asked.

Neighbour Agnes Wharton,[73] who had lived in the cellar of 5 Skirving Street, remembered Maggie being taken ill. After the doctor's first visit she went in to see Maggie, finding her in bed in Mrs Flanagan's bedroom. She and Catherine Flanagan then went for a drink together in the local public house. She said to Catherine, 'I'm sorry to see poor Maggie is ill' to which Flanagan replied, 'Oh, she'll never rise out of that bed.' Mrs Wharton protested, 'While there is life there is hope.' Mrs Flanagan, however, was pessimistic and predicted, 'No, she'll never live to comb a grey hair'. Mrs Flanagan told Mrs Wharton that Maggie had been ill several times before, yet her father had specifically said in his evidence at the committal that she had only had one illness, two years earlier, and was otherwise a healthy girl.[74] Indeed, both Mrs Wharton and Dr Rafter agreed that the girl looked healthy. However, it no doubt suited Catherine Flanagan to say otherwise. Mrs Wharton sent some grapes and oranges in for Maggie, but when she next visited Maggie and asked if she had got the fruit, she said that Mrs Flanagan told her 'not to buy her any more as I was poor and she had plenty of those things'. Mrs Wharton confirms that both sisters gave Maggie drinks. When Mrs Wharton had finished, her evidence-in-chief, Mr Neale, solicitor for Mrs Flanagan, asked her about Mrs Flanagan's treatment of Maggie. Mrs Wharton replied that Maggie 'never made any complaint of Mrs Flanagan's treatment. So far as I know Mrs Flanagan treated her kindly.' Re-examined by the prosecuting solicitor, she expanded that remark, saying, 'I never had any conversation with the girl alone during her illness as Mrs Flanagan was always in the room.'[75] No chance, then, was taken.

Both sisters were committed on this murder. Maggie's brother Patrick gave evidence to the coroner about her last hours.[76] Both sisters were attending Maggie in the parlour and both came out together, Mrs Higgins carrying a cup in her hand. She said, 'Maggie won't last the night.' Thomas Higgins then came downstairs and asked how Maggie was; Mrs Flanagan answered, 'She is very low.' Thomas Higgins then went in to the parlour to see her, and when he came out said to young Patrick, 'Either you or your father should sit up with Maggie tonight,' whereupon 'Mrs Flanagan turned round and with a vulgar word said, "What should he or his father sit up with her for?"'

Maggie did indeed die without her father and brother being with her. Her father, when giving evidence at the committal proceedings relating to her death, said:[77]

> I was in the house when my daughter died. The prisoners came into the kitchen to inform me she was dead and took me into the room. I did not think she was likely to die. I had insured my daughter in the Scottish Legal Assurance Company eight or nine months before.[78] I came home one evening from work about that time and Mrs Flanagan and the club man persuaded me to it. For a time Mrs Flanagan paid for me the 2d. a week and I paid her back but latterly I forgot it altogether and Mrs Flanagan kept up the payments and I did not pay her back.

With hindsight there are obvious reasons why Mrs Flanagan would not want the policy to lapse. As the local collector for the company, George Griffiths, said in evidence in answer to a question from Mr Neale, solicitor for Flanagan:[79] 'I don't remember Mrs Flanagan complaining of having to pay this premium' (she wouldn't, would she!). I suspect that Mr Neale was anticipating a different answer, or he would not have asked that question.

After Maggie died Mrs Flanagan urged Patrick to go and collect the insurance money. Accompanied by Ellen Flanagan, Catherine's thirteen-year-old literate daughter, they attended at the office of the Registrar, obtaining a death certificate naming Mrs Flanagan as informant and 'aunt'.[80]

From there they went to the Scottish Legal Assurance Company office. On being told there was a delay, Mrs Flanagan then suggested they '... go up as far as the Liver and see what we can do there.' Patrick adds: 'At that time I did not know my daughter was insured in the Liver.' Indeed, there was no reason why he would have known about that insurance. According to the proposal form[81] Maggie's parents were both dead, she had 'neither brothers nor sisters, only one brother in

(Copy Document marked I 11)

Royal Liver Friendly Society.
PROPOSAL FORM
FOR
Assurances under Table 4, Schedule B, payable at Death.

District of *Liverpool* Agent

Canvasser Collector *P Dolan*

PARTICULARS OF ASSURANCE NOW PROPOSED.

Table No	Date of Proposal	Age next birthday	Pay every 4th week	Sum assured			If an increase, insert here the word "Increase."
				£	s.	d.	
4.	2/11/82	18 years	1/4	50	—	—	

QUESTIONS to be Answered by the Person on whose Life the Assurance is proposed:—

1.—What is your Name and Address? (NAME) *Margaret Jennings* (ADDRESS) *37 Blenheim St*

2.—What is your Profession, or Occupation? *Spinster*

3.—What will be your Age next birthday?

4.—(A) Are you already insured in this Society? (A) *No*
(B) If so, what is the total amount? (B)
(C) What is the name of Collector? (C)

5.—(A) Have you been, or are you afflicted with Rupture, Gout, Dropsy, Palsy, Asthma, Insanity, Spitting of Blood, or with an habitual cough, Disease of the Lungs, or with any other Disease, Disorder, Affliction, or Complaint tending to shorten life? (A) *No*
(B) Are you subject to Fits? (B)

6.—Have your Parents, Brothers, or Sisters, been Healthy, and long-lived, or otherwise? *Cannot say*

7.—If any have died, state the cause of Death, and at what age they respectively died? *Parents dead. Have neither brothers nor sisters — only one brother in the army, supposed to be dead.*

8.—(A) When were you last ill? (B) What was the nature of your illness? (A) *Was never ill* (B)

9.—Are you now in good Health? *Yes*

10.—What is the Name and Address of your usual Medical Attendant, to be referred to if necessary? Has known me *None* years.

11.—Have you ever been rejected by this or any other Friendly Society, or Assurance Company? *No*

12.—Is there any other circumstance or information, touching your past or present Health, or habits of Life, with which the Committee of Management ought to be made acquainted?

DECLARATION.

I, *Catherine Flanagan* being desirous of effecting an Assurance with the ROYAL LIVER FRIENDLY SOCIETY, under Table 4, Schedule B, for the sum of £ *50* on the life of *Margaret Jennings* payable at Death, do hereby consent to pay EVERY FOURTH WEEK for the above sum; and do hereby declare that the Answers to the above Questions are true, to the best of my knowledge and belief, and I agree that the Questions and Answers, taken together, shall be the basis of the Contract between the said Society and me, and that, if any false statement or misrepresentation be contained in any of the said Answers, or if there be any wilful omission therein, or concealment of any fact which ought to be made known to the Committee of Management of the said Society, or if the referees have knowingly given false testimonials, all moneys paid to the Society on account of such Assurance shall be forfeited, and the Assurance itself shall be null and void to all intents and purposes. And I do further agree that the Assurance hereby proposed shall not be binding on the Society until the delivery of a Policy on the said life, in conformity with the Rules and Regulations of the said Society.

her aunt

Signature (or mark) of proposed Member, or the person acting on his or her behalf { If person signing on behalf of Assurer be a relative, degree of relationship must be stated; also address. } *Catherine Flanagan her X mark 37 Blenheim St.*

Witness { Agent, Collector, or Canvasser to sign here } *P Dolan*

Address *2 in 5 Ct Hunter St* Date *October 2nd* 1882

A Member not being under the age of 16 years, may nominate, in accordance with Act of Parliament, any person not being an Officer or Servant of the Society, to receive the amount due on this Insurance. Forms for same may be obtained through the Agent.

Margaret Jennings' insurance proposal form.

the army, supposed to be dead.' Further, Catherine put her mark on
the form as 'aunt'. As Catherine Flanagan knew full well, Maggie was
not related to her in any way and had both father and brother alive
(Patrick Jennings the elder lived with her, and her brother, also Patrick,
a bricklayer aged about 20, lived nearby at 24 Richmond Row). Note
also that in answer to the question on the form about health is written
'was never ill',[82] contrary to Flanagan's comment to Mrs Wharton when
they were discussing Maggie's health.

They duly went to the Liver, Mrs Flanagan handing Patrick some
documents en route and telling him to 'put them on the counter and
give them to Mr Whitehead'. Unfortunately for them, the amount of £50
that was due to them could not be paid out until probate of the estate
of the deceased had been obtained.

The three of them took the necessary documentation to the Probate
Court and Mrs Flanagan handed Patrick 15s. in respect of the fee. A few
days later 'we three' went back to the office of the 'Scottish Legal' and
Patrick duly received and made his mark for £9.[83] Mrs Flanagan said
she had had to borrow money to bury the girl, so Patrick gave her £8
10s., keeping 10s. for himself. A few days later Patrick, Mrs Flanagan,
her son and daughter went to the Probate Court, collected the necessary
documentation, walked to the offices of the Royal Liver Insurance
Company and Patrick was paid £50 'in notes'. Patrick continues:

> We went to a Bank in Castle Street and got the notes changed.
> I gave Mrs Flanagan £32 and her daughter a sovereign and kept
> £17 myself. I did not go back to Mrs Flanagan's house as I was
> afraid of Mrs Flanagan and her son, that the son might beat me
> and take the £17. Mrs Flanagan had told me that if I gave her the
> £50 she would buy me a pony and cart.

He declined the offer. According to the report of the committal
proceedings in the Liverpool Echo[84] the money was paid out under the
arch of the Police Court (the irony of the venue causing laughter in
court). In a separate article in the Liverpool Echo of 11 October 1883,
Patrick Jennings told the reporter about his daughter's illness and death.
This was published during the period before the inquest on Maggie and
while Catherine Flanagan was still on the run from the police. Jennings
says he took the advice of Patrick Higgins (brother of Thomas who was
then still alive) about the number of insurances taken out on Maggie

by Catherine Flanagan. Patrick Higgins advised him to take out letters of administration. He told the reporter that he did so but when he went to draw out the money, Mrs Flanagan and her daughter followed him 'like detectives'. Thus there is some slight difference from the evidence Patrick Jennings gave on oath, but it is not of any great importance. Indeed if he did actually make those comments to Patrick Higgins they may have been the clues that made the latter suspicious when his brother Thomas died.

After Margaret Jennings' body had been exhumed, it fell to Patrick,[85] his son,[86] and Mrs Wharton[87] to identify her body. They did so, her father adding wistfully, 'I was not aware the deceased was buried in a public grave, Catherine Flanagan did all herself and paid for all.'[88]

Maggie had buried at Ford Cemetery on 28 January 1883. Following a request from Mr Marks, the Liverpool prosecuting solicitor,[89] an exhumation took place on 16 November 1883 and after the post-mortem examination her body was reinterred in the same public grave.[90] Dr Lowndes conducted the post-mortem examination.[91] His evidence, coupled with that of the eminent analytical chemist Edward Davies[92] and Professor James Campbell Brown,[93] left no doubt that Margaret Jennings had been poisoned by arsenic. Dr Lowndes[94] noted that outwardly there was considerable decomposition of the body but the internal organs and intestines were 'very well preserved'. There were 'some indications of an irritant poison in the intestines'. Her lungs were too decomposed to allow 'opinion being found as to their condition at time of death', but the body was in a much better state of preservation than expected of a body buried some ten months earlier. He commented that 'arsenic would have a preservative effect upon the body generally but upon the intestines primarily.' Edward Davies, the chemist assigned to the case, conducted chemical tests on various parts of the intestines and organs which showed presence of arsenic.[95]

In her statement, Catherine Flanagan blames her sister for Maggie's death, saying: 'Higgins administered the poison which killed Margaret Jennings.[96] She always obtained the papers and mixed and administered the poison and got me to make the assurances and attend the people until they died.'

Maria Hoare in her statement to the press alleged there was plenty of gossip about poison in the neighbourhood at the time of Maggie's death.[97] The Liverpool Echo on 19 October 1883 recorded her as saying 'and when the girl Jennings was buried expressions were used that there had been poisoning going on ...'

Mrs Hoare went on to say that Mrs Flanagan (and therefore Margaret Higgins and the rest of the lodgers as well, although Maria Hoare does not point that out) moved out of Skirving Street the following week and went to live in Latimer Street. She presses the point home, adding further: 'Whenever some of the people she had insured died, she sometimes changed her residence.'

Other insurances were taken out on Maggie's life, apart from the policies with the Liver and the Scottish Legal. On 15 May 1882 a policy was taken out with the British Workmen's Insurance Company.[98] Catherine proposed her life, with Margaret Higgins present at the time. The sum was for £19 16s. 0d. Mrs Flanagan paid some of the premiums, and £19 10s. 6d. was duly paid out to Catherine Flanagan on 8 February 1883.

Another policy was taken out with the Crown and Anchor Assurance and Burial Society.[99] Mr Howley, the collector, received a verbal proposal on 28 October 1882 from Mrs Stanton. He explained that for sums under £25 no written proposal was required. Mrs Stanton told him the policy was for the benefit of the aunt of the girl, no name being given. The sum assured was £24 12s. 0d. The clerk, Mr John Smith,[100] told the coroner that only thirteen weeks' premiums had been paid by the time Maggie died. Mrs Flanagan and another woman called to claim the benefit of the policy on the death of her 'niece', saying that she was in great trouble and had not sufficient money to bury the body. (It is not made clear by Mr Smith but one assumes that the policy was somehow voided by the lack of premiums paid.) Moved by 'her plea of poverty', a grant of 10s. was paid to Mrs Flanagan.

Probably the most chilling moment comes when Patrick Dolan, a collector for the Royal Liver Friendly Society,[101] visited Mrs Flanagan at 31 Blenheim Street on 2 October 1882. He was collecting other premiums and in the course of conversation, 'Mrs Flanagan said she had heard we had a new rule in the society and she would like to know the terms of it. I told her. She then said she thought she had another member for me and wanted to know the terms per month for a person eighteen years of age on £50. I asked who the person was and she said "It's Maggie". Maggie Jennings was working in the kitchen at the time and she turned round to me and smiled.' Minutes later, Maggie's death warrant in the shape of the proposal form was signed as Mrs Flanagan made her mark as Maggie's 'aunt'. As Mr Dolan bluntly states: 'The proposal was accepted on 9 October 1882. The girl died on 25 January following.' His full statement is below.

Statement of Patrick Dolan, taken on Oath before the Liverpool City Coroner, 11 January 1884 at the Inquest into the death of Margaret Jennings.

PATRICK DOLAN being sworn says:

I am a collector for the Royal Liver Friendly Society. I live in 2 House, 5 Court, Hunter Street Liverpool.

I know the two women, Mrs Flanagan and Mrs Higgins now in custody. I knew the deceased Margaret Jennings. Her life was insured in our Society. She was proposed by Mrs Flanagan. I took the proposal myself, it was by Mrs Flanagan. I remember on 2 October 1882 calling upon Mrs Flanagan at 31 Blenheim Street about the premiums on another policy. In the course of conversation Mrs Flanagan said she had heard we had a new rule in the society and she would like to know the terms of it and I told her. She then said she thought she had another member for me and wanted to know the terms per month for a person eighteen years of age on £50. I asked who the person was and she said 'It's Maggie'. Maggie Jennings was working in the kitchen at the time and she turned round to me and smiled. I filled the proposal up and had to get some one to sign it. Mrs Flanagan put her mark to it and said she was the girl's 'Aunt'. The proposal was accepted on 9 October 1882. The girl died on 25 January following. The first step in making a claim is the production of a certificate of death. A claim was made under this policy by Mrs Flanagan and Patrick Jennings the father of the deceased. When the proposal was made I enquired of Mrs Flanagan had she any other relatives and she said 'No she had no one alive' she said she was the only relative living. About a week before the deceased girl died I remember Mrs Flanagan said to me in Scotland Road that Maggie was seriously ill and that she (Mrs Flanagan) was very sorry she did not get a nomination form before that in favour of herself in case Maggie should die as she was beginning to think the father would lay claim to the fifty

pounds. I had forgotten then that she had stated that she was the
only relation. I told her I would give her a nomination paper at
any time by payment of 1s. the usual fee, I asked her then if she
would pay the 1s. and I would send the form in the usual way.
She did not give me the 1s. and the next I heard was that the girl
Maggie was dead. A day or two after the death Mrs Flanagan was
at our office with a man.

Patrick Dolan

Sworn before me,

Clarke Aspinall, Coroner of Liverpool

The total insurance on Maggie's life amounted to £112 8s. 0d. but netted
only £79. With burial in a public grave, the profit was nevertheless
considerable.

Both women were committed on this murder charge and the evidence
does support joint culpability.[102]

John Flanagan

The fourth victim whose death was considered as part of the 'similar
fact' evidence at the trial was that of John Flanagan, Catherine's son. He
died, aged 22, at 142 Blenheim Street on 7 December 1880 and, like the
other victims, was buried in a public grave at Ford Cemetery. Permission
was given for his body to be exhumed[103] on 16 January 1884.[104] Maria
Hoare made a statement to the Liverpool Echo[105] saying that he 'was only
entered in clubs about 10 weeks before his death'. At the committal
proceedings[106] Mrs Hoare repeated a conversation she had had with
Catherine Flanagan which is reminiscent of the exchange Catherine had
with Mrs Wharton[107] concerning Maggie Jennings' health.'She said her
son John was very ill, that he was like the Flanagans very consumptive
and would go off like the rest and he would not comb a grey head.' And
later: 'She said he was very bad and would do no good. I said he was
very young and might recover. She shook her head and said "Oh, no,
he'll do no good".' Certainly Dr Hill was content to certify[108] the cause
of death as bronchitis so his mother's predictions came true. In view of
the result of the post-mortem examination on his exhumed body, it is
clear why she was so certain he would not recover. Dr Whitford stated[109]
that his body 'was in a state of very remarkable preservation considering
the time it had been buried' (three years) and completely overturned

Dr Hill's diagnosis of bronchitis by stating 'there were no pleural adhesions or any indications of disease ... there were no indications of bronchitis.' Dr Lowndes agreed with Dr Whitford, noting from his own observations of the exhumed body that the heart and lungs were 'healthy and well preserved'.[110] It will come as no surprise that Edward Davies, the chemist, found 'large quantities of arsenic in liver spleen kidneys and intestines'.[111]

John Flanagan's death had formed part of the allegation by Mrs Hoare that Flanagan 'had poisoned her husband and son', to which Catherine took so much exception that she instituted and won an action for slander. During the committal proceedings, the solicitor for Flanagan asked about Mrs Hoare's relationship with his client. Her answer was that she had not been 'on good terms' with her 'and I did not wish to be as I heard her sister throwing this poisoning case into her face. She brought an action against me for slander and got damages, £5 and costs. I have paid £10 of it. I have never spoken to her since.' As Mr Neale sank back onto the advocates' bench the prosecuting solicitor, Mr Marks, then rose to his feet to cross-examine and elicited the evidence: 'The slander was

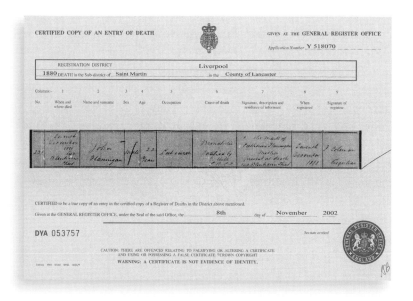

The death certificate of John Flanagan recorded the cause of death
as Bronchitis.

for saying she had poisoned her son and her husband.'[112] The judge, Mr Justice Butt, strictly controlled Mrs Hoare's evidence at the trial, and this statement was not repeated before the jury.[113] (They had had the opportunity to read her 'interesting statement'[114] in the *Liverpool Echo* on 19 October 1883 in any event.)

In her statement Flanagan says: 'My son John followed and he was insured by me but Higgins poisoned him and got a share of the money.'[115] It is interesting that Flanagan does not condemn Higgins for killing her son; indeed, the sharing of the insurance money indicates complicity.

John Flanagan was insured in five different societies, for a total of £95 10s. 0d.

In or around June 1879 Catherine started paying premiums to John Gwynne, an agent for the Prudential Assurance Company.[116] The sum assured was £24 18s. 0d.[117] and Catherine claimed and was paid the full amount when her son died.[118] The Victoria Legal Society[119] policy[120] was originally taken out by John's wife, who also insured herself, encouraged by Catherine to take out the two policies. Mr Hoolihan, the agent, stated that John was not present when the proposal was made. When the wife died, Catherine kept up the payments and in October 1879 she increased the payments from 1d. per week to 3d. per week, for a sum assured of £23 2s. 0d. The benefit paid to Catherine was £15.[121]

The Pearl Life Policy netted Catherine only £3 16s. 0d., paid as half benefit[122] (usually half benefit was paid when the policy has been in existence for less than twelve months), although the original sum was for £7 16s. 0d.[123]

The Liverpool Protective Burial Society insured John for £24. The sum of £12 as half benefit was duly paid on John's death.[124]

The last policy on John's life was taken out with the Wesleyan and General Assurance Company (I know not by whom) on 3 September 1880 for the sum of £15 14s. Catherine paid the premiums and was duly paid the full sum when he died[125] just three months later on 7 December.[126]

In all, £56 8s. 0d. was paid out and the sisters were found to be jointly responsible for this murder.[127]

GROUP TWO

There is less direct evidence for the second group of six deaths but some background information about the victims can be gleaned from the letters and reports which swell the file at the Public Record Office.[128] The prosecuting solicitor for Liverpool, William Marks, had instructed the police to investigate the matters raised by Mrs Flanagan in her statement.[129] (This statement was made to her solicitor before her onviction, although not dated.) She admitted that she knew that certain people were being poisoned but denied ever administering it herself, being only involved in the obtaining of insurance. She blamed four other women: Margaret Evans, Catherine Ryan, Mrs Begley and her co-accused Margaret Higgins.

Marks came to the conclusion that while it was probable that the six named 'extra' victims were poisoned, it would be very difficult to secure a conviction against any other person unless they could prove that neither of the two sisters had access to the victim. He considered the prospect of bringing a prosecution against anyone else unrealistic. He informed the DPP that Flanagan's solicitor had approached him before the trial, offering his client's willingness to give evidence for the crown, clearly with a view to securing clemency. This offer had been declined. All cases, except that of a boy called Charles Mure, were known to the police prior to Catherine Flanagan's statement.[130]

Mary Donnelly (Snr)

Mary Donnelly died on 7 February 1879, aged 47, while living at 2 Court, St Martin Street; she was buried at Ford Cemetery two days later in a public grave.[131] She lived in the same house as the sisters so each of them would have had the opportunity to administer poison.[132] Flanagan, however, accuses her sister of the deed, acting alone, and indicated that she was insured 'by a good few' including her own daughter who later gave Higgins £10.[133] That daughter, also Mary Donnelly, who was soon to marry John Flanagan, Catherine's son, was present at her mother's death, according to the death certificate. The cause of her demise was certified by Dr H.F. Fisher as being bronchitis.[134]

Apparently this death was one of those previously known by police even before the statement was tendered.[135] According to Maria Hoare, whose dislike of Mrs Flanagan was only matched by her enthusiasm

The death certificate of Mary Donnelly (Snr).

for making malicious statements about her, 'there was a great deal of talk about the neighbourhood about her relations and acquaintances dying, for it was known they were entered into so many societies. After one of her friends, a girl named Donnelly died, there was shouting in the streets when the funeral took place ...'[136] It is possible that she was murdered but impossible to say by whom or whether one or both sisters were involved.

Mary Donnelly (Jnr)

Mary Donnelly was followed a year later by her daughter, 20-year-old Mary (who had married John Flanagan during that short period), who died on 6 February 1880 at 8 Epsom Street and was buried at Ford Cemetery in a public grave on 8 Feb 1880.[137] Her death was certified by Dr J. Utting as being due to 'Pneumonia, twenty-one days' and Catherine Flanagan, her mother-in-law, was present at her death.[138]

She was the wife of Catherine's son John, who had insured her life with the Prudential Society and drew £20 on her death.[139] In her statement Catherine names Margaret Higgins as the poisoner, she being given £4 from the insurance money by the new widower.[140] Both sisters

The death certificate of Mary Donnelly (Jnr).

had access to her and thus the opportunity to administer poison as they all lived in the same house[141] in Epsom Street.[142] This case was previously known to police.[143] Apart from the statement by Catherine, there was evidence given at the committal proceedings concerning the death of John Flanagan that his late wife had been insured.[144]

It was rumoured locally that she was murdered; she was insured and both sisters had the opportunity to poison her. There is a strong probability that she was murdered.

She in turn was followed by her husband John, Catherine's son, whose death on 7 December 1880 came into the first category of victims, evidence of his poisoning being given at the trial.

Emma Godfrey

Emma Godfrey died at the age of 31 on 22 October 1879 at 27 St Martin Street[145] and was buried at Ford Cemetery.[146] Flanagan accused Mrs Begley[147] of her murder but a Mrs MacNamara implicated Catherine Flanagan and, to a lesser degree, Mrs Begley. The police were already aware of this allegation prior to Flanagan's statement being made available to them.[148]

The two police officers assigned to deal with the case as a whole were Inspectors Boyes and Maxwell. Police Inspector Stephen Boyes was aged 38 when the 1881 census was compiled. He was born in Scotland and lived at 14 Lloyd Street, Everton with five Liverpudlian children, his Devon-born wife and her sister.

His colleague, Inspector Edwin Maxwell, was Irish and lived at 36 Powis Street, Toxteth Park. The census gives his age as 31. His family consisted of his wife, three children and his brother (also a policeman) and sister.

Catherine Flanagan refers to the death in her statement[149] saying that Emma Godfrey died at Owen Begley's in St Martin Street.[150] (According to the 1881 census of Liverpool, she is listed at 34 St Martin Street living with her husband Owen, a dock labourer aged 40. Bridget's age is given as 42. Both were born in Ireland. In the house next door lived Catherine Ryan, of whom more later.)

Catherine Flanagan admitted being joint insurer of Emma Godfrey with Mrs Begley, and alleged that 'Mrs Begley knew what was used to kill and I have seen her mix and administer the poison to Godfrey who died soon afterwards.'[151] Flanagan does not connect Higgins with this death at all. Inspector Stephen Boyes[152] confirmed that Godfrey was lodging with Bridget Begley when she died, having been attended by Dr Houlgrave who certified the cause of death as paralysis. She earned her living selling matches in the street and was partly paralysed, but apart from that was in generally good health. Mrs MacNamara, who lived in the cellar under the Begley's house, told the police officer that she remembered the woman being taken ill and suffering greatly from purging and vomiting, the classic symptoms of arsenic poisoning. She further remembers her being visited by Catherine Flanagan and Mrs Begley and that she saw Mrs Flanagan put something into some port wine, which she gave to Godfrey who became violently ill afterwards. On another occasion when Flanagan visited Godfrey, she offered her a cup of tea and some tea cake but Godfrey only drank a little of the liquid. Mrs MacNamara's small daughter finished off the rest and was taken very ill on the street with vomiting and purging, being seriously ill for some days afterwards; fortunately she recovered. Mrs MacNamara did not give any evidence on oath and her statement was taken by the police officer investigating the matter. Nevertheless, it carries more credibility than an interview by a news reporter as it would have been taken in confidence and Mrs MacNamara would have been urged towards the truth rather than sensation.

Emma Godfrey died in agony according to Mrs MacNamara, who was with her at her death, having been asked to stay with the dying woman by Flanagan and Begley. According to the death certificate, Mrs Begley claimed to have been present at the death and falsely claimed to have been the cousin of the deceased.[153]

It is probably the case that Flanagan and Begley poisoned Godfrey but that Higgins was not involved in this case. The Treasury Solicitor[154] commented that it was an isolated case so far as Begley was concerned, and assuming that Godfrey was poisoned, a view to which he was inclined,[155] the only evidence against Begley apart from Flanagan's allegation would be that she and Godfrey lived in the same house. Flanagan was seen to give the tea and port wine, not Begley, and although all the symptoms pointed to poisoning, he came to the conclusion that there was no point taking the matter any further.

Maria Hoare buried Godfrey at the request of Flanagan and Begley. She told Inspector Boyes: 'Mr Whitehead of the Liver paid me. She was insured both by Flanagan and Begley. I heard she was poisoned.'[156] She went further in her statement to the *Liverpool Echo*[157] on 19 October 1883 (no doubt much to the delight of the reporter) saying that Godfrey 'sold matches on Burlington Bridge' and:

> 'Mrs Flanagan had Godfrey insured in the Royal Liver, Prudential and other societies and they got for her a kind of will. During her sickness Mrs Flanagan attended her. My husband and me buried Godfrey and Mrs Flanagan came to me afterwards and asked me to make out my bill and take it to the Royal Liver. I made out the bill, including in it a hearse, coach, coffin and ground but they would not pay me for more than two coaches. With this difference I received my money from the Liver for the undertaking expenses and afterwards Mrs Flanagan came to me and asked me to go to another club with her and make out another funeral bill for the deceased, get it paid as if I had not been to the Liver, and hand the money over to her. I said I would not do it, as it would be cheating, and that I had children, and was not going to get myself into trouble. She abused me, and said she would never come to me for another funeral, and we fell out. That was the last funeral I had from her.'

She later accused Flanagan to her face, saying: 'I was sure she had not done right to Godfrey and that she had given her a "dose too much".'

Mrs Hoare continued:

When the funeral of Godfrey was starting from St Martin Street I was in the house looking after the undertaking arrangements, and Mrs Flanagan asked me to have a drop of whisky out of a cup. I said I could not take it raw and a sup of tea was put in for me, and I took it. Directly afterwards I had a burning across my inside, and I felt unwell. She laughed when I told her about it. I felt bad afterwards for three weeks. I saw a doctor and he gave me a bottle of medicine.'

How far this is true one cannot tell; either it was a malicious attempt by Flanagan to hurt Mrs Hoare, or an attempt by Mrs Hoare to avenge the loss of the slander action. None of these comments, quite rightly, was allowed in evidence, but doubtless the jury would have read them in the newspaper in any event. However, leaving them aside, the inevitable conclusion must be that Godfrey was poisoned, probably by Flanagan.

Mrs Begley was not interviewed at all so her version of events is unknown but obviously she would have denied involvement. Certainly her close association with Flanagan when the latter was visiting the sick woman points to a joint enterprise between the two women, both being responsible for the death. Higgins had nothing to do with the case.[158]

Catherine Neillan

Catherine Neillan died on 4 April 1880[159] at the age of 51. She was buried on 7 April 1880 at Ford Cemetery in a public grave.[160]

At the time of her death she was lodging at 39 Kew Street with Margaret Evans[161] and Margaret Higgins was also lodging there. She was attended in her illness by Dr Fisher who had died by the time the police investigated her death, but he certified her cause of death as 'Morbis cordis'[162] (heart failure). Catherine Flanagan alleged in her statement that her sister told her that she and Evans poisoned Neillan. Margaret Evans obtained the poison, they both 'attended on her and they used Flypaper water'. She further says that Neillan was insured by both Evans and two other women, Margaret Potter and Mrs Fallon.[163]

Maria Hoare commented on Neillan's death in her statement to Inspector Boyes. She did not undertake the funeral and said that

Michael Darcy of Vauxhall Road attended to it instead. She did, however, remember the event and recalls there was a 'great deal of talk about her having been poisoned'. Mrs Fallon had told her she had had Neillan in a club 'but not long'. The length of time may correlate to Mrs Hoare's further comment that Neillan had been living in the Evans household for no longer than three months.[164]

There is nothing to link Flanagan with this death, and the evidence, taken on its own, is tenuous against Higgins and Evans. Circumstantially, however, suspicion lies heavy on both women when their involvement with other deaths is considered.[165]

Catherine O'Brien

Catherine O'Brien, the wife of Hugh, died aged 47 on 19 April 1882 at 3 House, 8 Court, Blenheim Street. In 1881 the census listed her and her husband at 49 Blenheim Street. She was then 46, he ten years younger. Both were Irish. Catherine Flanagan admitted[166] that she saw Evans make up some powder and give it to Catherine O'Brien, who died the following day. The woman was insured, allegedly by Flanagan, Evans, Stanton and Pugh, but there are no details or firm evidence. The doctor who attended her, Dr Hill,[167] was unable to recall any details which might have assisted the police investigation, having certified death as being due to 'paralysis and apoplexy'. Mary Carroll, Flanagan's sister-in-law, also visited this victim. The police suspected her generally of 'malpractice' but there was no evidence against her either in this or other cases and no direct accusation by Flanagan.

Margaret Higgins, according to her sister's statement, had no involvement in this death at all.

Charles Emmanuel Mure ('Mule')

Charles Emmanuel Mure died on 14 March 1883[168] aged 16 at 59 Conway Street, Seaforth, Liverpool. He is referred to in the police report[169] as 'an imbecile' living with his parents. His death was not previously noted by police and the first indication that he might have been murdered by poisoning came in the statement of Catherine Flanagan.[170]

While denying her own involvement she says that she was in a druggist's shop at the corner of Burlington Street when Catherine Ryan[171] got some poison, light blue in colour. She gave the packet to Flanagan to pass on to Margaret Evans,[172] which she did. Evans said to

Flanagan, 'I want money and I must have it and I am going to see a young fellow who is sick.' Flanagan thought the boy's name was 'Mule' or similar. Apparently 'Mule' died shortly after Evans' visit. Flanagan says she did not know 'what she (Evans) got by his death' (meaning insurance) but added: 'She (Evans) has his father in clubs.'[173]

The Mure family had apparently lived in the same house as Margaret Evans in Blenheim Street prior to moving to Seaforth some months before Charles died.[174]

Reading through the general correspondence about this case contained in the PRO file, there is clearly a conflict of opinion as to whether the boy was murdered or died through natural causes. The Treasury Solicitor, Mr Cuffe,[175] made an exploratory visit to Liverpool and interviewed the boy's father. He was aware of the insurance situation (which tends to confirm that Evans did have the lad insured) but nevertheless was disinclined to believe ill of Mrs Evans. The body was not exhumed and the doctor who attended Mure was less than helpful. Mr Cuffe interviewed Dr Brown during his visit, taking some rough notes of the doctor's recollection.[176] Mr Cuffe's note reads that the doctor recalled that 'it was a hopeless case from the first and the lad was dying and even when the possibility of poisoning was suggested to him by me he said that, looking back on the case, he could remember no symptoms consistent with that theory.' The doctor told him: "There was nothing in his state when I saw him to lead to any inference of poisoning ... I never saw him vomiting but was told he had been.' Mr Cuffe concluded that the boy was in a painless coma the day before he died and Dr Brown certainly seemed opposed to the theory that he was poisoned by arsenic.[177]

However, by the time Dr Brown had been seen by Inspector Boyes[178] he appeared to have changed his opinion. Dr Brown had certified the death as caused by 'coma consequent on water on the brain'. He told Inspector Boyes that the lad suffered from vomiting and purging which he originally thought was a consequence of water on the brain, but Inspector Boyes reported 'the doctor now appears to be of the opinion that it is probable that the death was from poisoning'. At which point Mr Cuffe appended in the margin of letter, seemingly irritated by the doctor's change of opinion, 'This is not what he says to me, see notes of conversation'.

Mr Cuffe reported that the father 'impressed me with his honesty, and having regard to Dr Brown's evidence I cannot think that this is a case of murder – but of course it may be – and the police evidently are inclined to think that it is.' Which takes us no further but emphasises the dilemma that this case caused.

However, the mother's statements to police [179] suggest that there may have been a sinister motive behind Mrs Evans' almost daily visits. Often the mother was sent on errands, leaving Charles alone with Mrs Evans, who was sometimes accompanied by Mrs Stanton. Mrs Evans frequently went to the scullery to fetch water for the boy to drink. On one occasion, fourteen days prior to his death, a visit by Mrs Evans resulted in the lad vomiting and purging that night. The police appear to have viewed Mure's death as murder but lacked sufficient evidence to prefer a charge. Whilst it can be proved that Mrs Evans visited frequently immediately prior to the lad's death, it cannot be shown either that she administered poison or, more importantly, that he died of such poisoning.

There was insufficient evidence to justify charging Mrs Evans despite suspicions. Inevitably, while Mure was clearly not destined for a long life, there are indications that Evans may have hastened his demise, and if indeed he was insured by her the suspicion is that much stronger.

Apart from the delivery of the blue powder there is no evidence to connect Mure's death with Flanagan and no connection with Higgins at all. The suspicion against Evans stems from her alleged conversation with Catherine Flanagan, the insurance on the boy's life, her association with Catherine Ryan and Mrs Stanton, and her attendance on the boy immediately prior to his death leading to symptoms of poisoning as described by his mother. So far as Evans is concerned, it is a case of 'much suspected, nothing proved'.[180]

GROUP THREE

So far as the third group is concerned, such evidence as exists is very difficult to evaluate, if indeed 'evidence' is the correct term to use as it consists of contemporary speculation and discussion. Inevitably any deaths occurring in the Flanagan household give rise to suspicions of malpractice and those suspicions are heightened by any suggestion that the deceased's life was insured. Accordingly those names should be mentioned and discussed as possible victims, if only for the sake of completeness, and I have listed them in chronological order of death.

In four of the cases there is no evidence of murder apart from Maria Hoare's allegations. However, she should not be dismissed lightly as a malicious gossip; her profession as an undertaker gave her credence and the police regarded her as a valuable informant.[181] Indeed, the Treasury Solicitor, Mr Cuffe, specifically commended her in a letter to the Home Office (PRO/7) saying 'she knows little but hears everything and has been and is likely to be very useful to the police'. Catherine Flanagan even referred to her in the statement she made to her solicitor; when naming the other women involved with the insurance aspects of the killings she said, 'Hoare knows them all'.

Catherine Flanagan's first husband

The details of the first husband of Catherine Flanagan cannot at present be ascertained. Indeed it has proved impossible to tell whether she had been married before she married John Flanagan. The only lead is the frequent occurrence of the name McCormick; for example she says at one stage she has a son called John McCormick and there is a family of that name living in the same house as Flanagan at the time of the 1881 census. It was one of the aliases she used when on the run from the police. Suspicion is fuelled by a press report[182] which refers to the first husband having been murdered, but this is probably best dismissed as salacious gossip.

Mrs Bridget Jennings

Bridget Jennings died on 29 September 1877 at 22 St Martin Street. She was the wife of Patrick Jennings and mother of Maggie. She is one of the two additional people whose deaths have been included in Group

Three for the sake of thoroughness. Patrick Jennings gave evidence about his daughter's death at her inquest on 17 November 1883, adding that his wife died 'about six years ago. She was bad for a long time'.[183] This comment would be reasonable in view of the cause of death as 'consumption'. On 2 January 1884 at the committal relating to Maggie's murder, Patrick added that he, his wife and Maggie had lodged with Mrs Flanagan for about twelve years.[184] That evidence does not give rise to any suspicions of murder; indeed, the late Mrs Jennings appears to have survived six years under Flanagan's roof. However, prior to the court appearances, Patrick Jennings was interviewed by a reporter from the *Liverpool Echo* and the comment there, taken in isolation, does give rise to a suspicion.[185] He stated that he and his wife had lodged with Mrs Flanagan but then added: 'My wife died soon after I went to live with Mrs Flanagan in Skirving Street' and, more ominously, 'I learned she [Catherine Flanagan] had insured my wife for £16 [this might be £10, the writing is unclear] and I taxed her with it but she denied it although I afterwards ascertained that she had done so.' However, being reasonable, it seems that the Jennings family had lived with Flanagan in various different houses and Mrs Jennings died shortly after they

The death certificate of Bridget Jennings.

THE BLACK WIDOWS OF LIVERPOOL

all moved to Skirving Street. In fact, Patrick made an error: his wife died at 22 St Martin Street, not Skirving Street, but after six years and a number of moves, one can hardly be too critical. The *Liverpool Post* merely commented the next day[186] that the late Mrs Jennings had died in Flanagan's house. There is no mention of Mrs Jennings' death elsewhere, and she was never considered to have been one of the other possible victims when the police conducted their detailed enquiry. There is no evidence that she was murdered but inevitably the death of anyone within the Flanagan household will, with the benefit of hindsight, attract suspicion that the demise was not from natural causes, especially if that person's life was insured by Flanagan. If she was terminally ill, it is possible that her life was insured as a short-term investment; the worst construction would be that she was 'hastened on her way'.

For the sake of completeness it must be said that Dr Fisher, who gave the cause of Mrs Jennings' death as consumption, had certified Catherine Neillan's death as due to 'morbis cordis' (in fact Catherine Flanagan's statement makes it clear she was poisoned and the police agreed), and Mary Donnelly's death as being due to bronchitis. It was agreed by all that she too had been poisoned. However, taking all things together there is no actual evidence of malpractice here and my conclusion is that she was not a victim. Perhaps Mrs Flanagan took advantage of the woman's inevitable death as an easy insurance investment.

Michael Flanagan

Michael Flanagan was Catherine Flanagan's brother-in-law and died between 1877 and 1881. Maria Hoare, in her interview with the *Echo*,[187] said: 'I remember Mr Flanagan's brother Michael dying also – he being also insured.' Once again, there is no evidence of murder, just an uneasy suspicion simply because of the relationship and the allegation of a pecuniary motive. The only burial of a man of that name at the right time is in a private grave at Ford Cemetery on 16 October 1879. He was aged 54 from 5 Overbury Street. It is not in the area I would expect and it is unlikely to be the correct person. This name is best dismissed from the list of probable victims.

Joseph Thompson

Joseph Thompson was the first husband of Margaret Higgins. According to Maria Hoare he died about 1877/78.[188] When giving evidence at

committal proceedings[189] she repeated the conversation she had
overheard between the two sisters, in which Margaret Higgins said to
Catherine Flanagan, 'You have poisoned my husband' and Flanagan
responded, 'He wasn't your husband, he was your fancy man. He was
an old Orangeman.'

This is slightly altered in a report in the *Liverpool Echo* on 19 October
1883[190] to: 'You have poisoned my husband'; 'What about him, he was
only an old Orangeman'; but the meaning is the same. It appears that
at one stage Mrs Hoare spread gossip that Mrs Flanagan had poisoned
her son and her husband. This fact was elicited at those committal
proceedings in explanation as to why she and Catherine were no longer
on friendly terms.[191] Catherine Flanagan had resented this allegation so
much that she brought an action for slander against Maria and James
Hoare[192] which she won, being awarded £5 damages and, according to
Mrs Hoare's evidence before the coroner,[193] costs as well. Mrs Hoare's
revenge came later, however, and the reporters from the local press
avidly took down her version of the quarrel and published it[194] on 19
October in the *Liverpool Echo*, prior to the trial under the heading 'Mrs
Hoare's Interesting Statement'. (This headline was probably the best
understatement of that year!) Mr Neale, Flanagan's solicitor, was furious
and complained both to the press and the stipendiary magistrate who
was hearing the final remands before the sisters were committed to their
trial. Alas, his complaints fell on stony ground.

The 'Interesting Statement' described how the two women fell out
over Mrs Hoare's refusal to deceive an insurance company. Then Mrs
Flanagan asked her to undertake another funeral for her, but she refused.
Mrs Hoare told the reporter:

> ... she said 'All right. I will it make it dear on you.' I met her
> in Scotland Road about three months afterwards and I was in
> company with a woman named Mrs Casey. Mrs Flanagan stopped
> us at the top of Horatio Street and began to abuse me. She aimed
> a blow at me with a basket and then Mrs Casey struck her, and I
> walked on, saying, 'Go away you wretch, you will be hung yet; a
> bad end will become of you.' Or something like that. I think I did
> say that I was sure she had not done right to Godfrey and that she
> had given her a 'dose too much'. I did not see her until Mr Ponton,
> her solicitor, sent me a letter asking to write an apology. I refused

to do so and another letter was sent to me and this I took no notice of. Then a writ was served upon me and my husband and I took it to Mr Quelch. The trial followed, Mrs Flanagan called Bridget O'Hare of Hornby Street; Margaret Evans, Blenheim Street; Owen Begley, St Martin Street; Mrs Potter, Tenterden Street; Mary Ann Husban, St Martin Street; and Patrick Flanagan her husband's cousin to swear that I said she had poisoned her husband and two sons and yet none of these people had been present in Scotland Road when me and Mrs Flanagan fell out. I brought two witnesses but the case went against me and I had to pay £5 damages. The costs and the damages came to between £39 and £40 and we had the bailiffs in our house a week nearly.

Mrs Hoare may have denied that she had made that allegation in Scotland Road but earlier in the same news report she told the reporter that she had known Catherine Flanagan for about seventeen years, had buried her husband John and two of her sons, John and Steven, along with Mr Flanagan's brother Michael, all of whom were insured. She also refers to burying 'several of her friends and acquaintances whose names I cannot recollect'. Emphasising how commonplace the practice was she stated 'It is a practice to put people in clubs unknown to themselves and one of Mrs Flanagan's friends now pays £1 a week in burial money, drawing the insurances as the people she enters die one by one.'

No wonder the defending solicitor was incensed.

Mrs Hoare says Joseph Thompson was insured, and that she did not undertake the funeral; it was dealt with by Brumby's. There is no record of his burial at Ford Cemetery,[195] which accords with him not being Roman Catholic. All efforts to trace his death and burial have failed.

There is no evidence of malpractice here, but heavy suspicion.

Stephen Flanagan

Stephen Flanagan (spelt Flannigan on his death certificate) was another son of Catherine and died at 23 St Martin's Street on 6 November 1878. His death was certified by Dr H. F. Fisher as being due to 'Bronchitis and Diarrhoea'. His mother, Catherine, was present at his death and duly made her mark on the certificate.

The only reference to his having been murdered comes from Maria Hoare when she said: '... Stephen Flanagan, another son who died two

The death certificate of Stephen 'Flannigan'.

years before his brother and was insured too.'[196] There is no evidence of murder, yet the symptom of diarrhoea is very typical of arsenic poisoning. In addition, the diagnosis of bronchitis did feature on a number of other death certificates where poisoning was proved to have taken place (Mary Higgins, John Flanagan Junior, Mary Donnelly).

His death, at so young an age, with those symptoms, added to Maria Hoare's allegations, must rank pretty high in the order of suspicious deaths.

John Flanagan Senior

John Flanagan Senior was the husband of Catherine and died of pneumonia on Midsummer's Day, 24 June 1879. He was 42 and buried in a public grave at Ford Cemetery on 29 June 1879. He was described as a 'Laborer' [sic] the cause of death 'pleuro pneumonia fourteen days' certified by R. O'Leary, MRCS. It was pneumonia that Dr Rafter mistakenly thought was the cause of Maggie Jenning's death. Young Mary Flanagan, according to Dr Utting, succumbed to the same illness at the age of 20. Could Dr O'Leary have been mistaken as well? Catherine Flanagan made her cross in the appropriate box as widow 'present at

The death certificate of John Flanagan.

death'. The address at 22 St Martin Street where he died was a house at some time inhabited by Mrs Evans (if my trace of her in the 1871 census is correct).[197] Additionally, both Mrs Ryan and the Begley family lived in that street according to the 1881 census, and the street was not unaccustomed to the funeral hearses appearing, other suspicious having deaths occurred there. Mrs Jennings died at No. 22, Emma Godfrey at No. 27 and Mary Donnelly at No. 2 Court.

John Flanagan senior was about ten years younger than Catherine, being only 21 when John Flanagan was born, and even younger should we suppose that Stephen was actually his son. In view of difference in age the thought of a first 'Mr Flanagan' becomes more of a possibility and given time more research may reap rewards.

The evidence of his murder, such as it is, comes from Maria Hoare at the committal proceedings relating to the charge of murder of John Flanagan junior.[198] She gave evidence of the slander action Catherine brought against her for saying 'she had poisoned her son and her husband'. In her statement to the press she says: 'about 4 years ago John Flanagan died, entered in several clubs and tontine societies' and said he was buried at Ford.[199] Patrick Higgins referred to him in passing as being a dock labourer, and thought he died 'about three years ago'.[200]

Apart from Maria Hoare, there is no evidence of murder but suspicion lingers, especially if we compare his cause of death with its date.

Thomas Higgins' first wife

Thomas Higgins' first wife died after the family moved into the Flanagan household. Exactly when that was is impossible to say, save that they were not included in the list of lodgers in the 1881 census. Nor, indeed, can they be found anywhere in Lancashire. The general impression gained is that they had not lived long with the sisters. Prosecuting counsel opening to jury at trial confirms that Thomas Higgins 'with his former wife, had lodged in the house or in the different houses in which Flanagan from time to time lived'.[201] Having checked the cemetery records and the St Catherine's Index for possible deaths of a suitable Mrs Higgins, I can find absolutely no trace of the lady at all.

There is no evidence of murder, but the seed of suspicion is planted because death occurred after moving to live in the sister's household, followed by the marriage of Thomas to Margaret and the prompt killing of the stepdaughter, Mary.

So far as these seven cases are concerned, there is no proof of unlawful killing. But had it not been for Patrick Higgins' suspicions leading to Dr Whitford's post-mortem examination of Thomas' body, there would have been no proof of that murder either. Nor would the other three bodies have been exhumed, nor would Catherine have made her statement confirming the poisoning of her list of six.

Ten murders.

Perhaps sufficient.

CHAPTER 3

⌘

Murderesses

Persons in their class of life have little knowledge of the property of
poisons and less ability to form a crafty scheme of crime.

Liverpool Echo

THE MORE I DELVED into the detail of these murders the more I
was struck by a rather startling truth. The Victorian image of a killer
was as an isolated figure, whose activities were only possible because
they separated themselves off from wider society. But far from working
alone these women appear to have been supported and sheltered by the
community in which they lived, whether by the turning of a blind eye
or by more direct abetting.

Was there a hidden dimension to the idea of the sharing, caring
working-class community? If anything could ease the misery and
deprivation of Liverpool slum dwellers in the 1880s it would surely
be the thought that their neighbours would stand by them in times of
exceptional hardship. But was there a dark side to the survival networks
which operated in Victorian working-class areas? The women, who
cried together, gossiped together, lent and borrowed and protected one
another: did they also kill together?

The word murderess itself speaks volumes. Society saw a difference
between men and women who murdered and the importance of the
victim was diminished by the revelation that the killer was a woman.

The pattern of public vilification of a female killer began in 1829 about
the time of the trial of Esther Hibner and became well established in the
decades that followed, gradually decreasing in the last twenty years of the
century. Multiple murders were more likely to be perpetrated by women

using poison, usually arsenic. Poison had long been the weapon of the women, who were in charge of a family's food and had the opportunity to add undesirable ingredients to someone's meal. Such was the public fear of these women that they were portrayed as monsters, whereas in reality they were ordinary but poor women, with nothing extraordinary about them to separate them from their peers.

There seemed to be an epidemic of poisoning cases in the 1840s when poverty was extreme. The legislators were well aware of the incentive the burial clubs provided and in the 1850s some of the legislative loopholes were closed by the Sale of Arsenic Act 1851. Burial clubs encouraged the poor to save money to pay for the funerals of their friends and relatives, so women found that they could make money over and above the cost of a funeral if they enrolled sickly candidates. Some went further, choosing healthy ones as well, as my research shows. The point will be made that poisoning for insurance money was widespread and of long standing.

Despite male disapproval, by the end of the nineteenth century women had acquired an appetite for murder trials. They went to court, wrote letters about injustice and generally 'interfered' in what men considered the male preserve of justice. As they ventured further into the public sphere their acquisition of knowledge was uncensored and acquired first-hand rather than filtered through their menfolk. The more they involved themselves the more they identified with the woman on trial and their presence and influence grew so as to be impossible to ignore.

After 1838, theft and fraud no longer attracted the death penalty so hangings became less frequent and perhaps thereby more of an occasion, taking on a carnival air. An executed woman was seen as an inhuman creature, and the hanging a ritual cleansing of society. There was a determination to distance the ideal woman of the home, the perfect, submissive, loving carer, from the woman in the dock. Thus by referring to her in terms which suggested she was unwomanly and bestial, mentally or physically deviant, the gulf was widened and society placated.

The Victorians had a fascination with and horror of women who committed crimes. They saw women as the moral fibre of the home, the bastions of respectability. Jurors, male and middle class, considered women either too pure, or more cynically, without the wit or strength to commit crime. Thus it went against their subconscious beliefs to

This photograph of the author's grandmother and great-grandmother typifies
the Victorian ideal of motherhood.

convict and they were less likely to return a guilty verdict. The reality was probably that women were convicted of less crime than men because they were not suspected.

Consequently, if a woman was convicted of a crime she had not only broken the law but also shattered the image of the perfect wife and mother. The sentence the court imposed was likely to be a harsher penalty than a man would receive, but the penalty for transgression of the social code was separate and additional to the sentence of the court and in effect more damning. Observers used vitriolic terms to condemn the female criminal, and only in the later part of the century did people start to realise that it was the social condemnation that prevented women from reforming rather than their own 'evil dispositions'.

The image of the murderess as a woman ostracised may be flawed if she stood not alone but with a group of like-minded neighbours. With the image of the Victorian deviant woman in mind, there are expectations of finding descriptions of the two sisters manipulated away from femininity and towards brutishness. The most fertile source of such descriptions has proved to be the local newspapers, which gave details of their physical appearance, their demeanour and their moral standards. Because of the extensive coverage of the crimes, the inquests and the criminal proceedings, it has been possible to monitor the attitude of the news reports to see if perspectives changed materially after conviction and if so, in what manner.

The fact that insurance policies were used to gain money was condemned both by the press and by the trial judge, but it was portrayed as very low-scale dishonesty and a despicable way of earning coppers,[1] rather than as the high-return investment that it clearly was. One policy[2] on the life of Maggie Jennings which had been operating for less than three months with a monthly premium of 1s. 4d. (7p in our terms) netted £50. The reward offered for the capture of Catherine Flanagan was £5.[3] In 1886 labourers in Liverpool would find only three or four days work each week, taking home about fifteen or sixteen shillings for the week (75p–80p).[4]

Advertisements in the local newspapers in October 1883 give good indications of the cost of living. Houses with six rooms were let for a weekly rent of 7s. 6d, umbrellas were advertised at between 1s. and 20s., a guinea would buy a wedding ring with a free set of six silver-plated teaspoons. Hyams' winter overcoats could be purchased from their Lord

List of Insurances

Thomas Higgins

Company	date taken out	amount insured	amount paid	date paid
British Workmen's Insurance Co.	18 Dec. 1882	£12 12s.	£12 9s. 6d.	4 Oct. 1883
Royal Liver Friendly Soc.	2 Apr. 1883	[£50]	(abortive attempt: TH said 'To hell with the clubs etc.')	
Scottish Legal Life Ass. Co.	10 Dec. 1882	about £15	£7 17s. 6d.	3 Oct. 1883
Pearl Life Ass. Co.[1]	March 1883	£40	Not paid	wrong body
Prudential Ass. Co.[2]	26 Feb. 1883	£15 12s.	£7 11s. 6d.	4 Oct. 1883
Wesleyan & Gen. Ass.Co.[3]	22 Feb. 1883	£25	£25	?
Totals		£108 4s.	£27 18s. 6d.	

Margaret Jennings

Company	date taken out	amount insured	amount paid	date paid
British Workmen's Insurance Co.[4]	15 May 1882	£19 16s.	£19 10s. 6d.	8 Feb. 1883
Scottish Legal Life Ass. Co.[5]	21 June ?	£18	£9	?
Crown & Anchor Ass. & Burial Soc.[6]	28 Oct 82	£24 12s.	10s.	
Royal Liver F. Soc.[7]	2 Oct. 1882	£50	£50	14 Feb 1883
Totals		£112 8s.	£79	

Mary Higgins

Company	date taken out	amount insured	amount paid	date paid
British Workmen's Assurance Co.[8]	9 Oct. 1882	£22 10s.	£21 18s. 6d.	2 Dec. 1882
Totals		£22 10s.	£21 18s. 6d.	

1. COR/TH F. D. Bowles & J. Bowles. taken out by MH & CF. EF signed TH for MH CF put hand out for policy which was given to her. CF paid first 3 premiums, MH paid rest. CF signed for pay out.
2. COR/TH Finnegan; taken out by CF pretending to be MH. Mrs Stanton paid some premiums. Paid out to CF pretending to be MH.
3. CTTL/TH D.Barr. no details but seems to have been paid.
4. COR/TH J.Williams. paid by CF, paid out to CF & MH.
5. COR/TH Griffiths & Cartright: CTTL/MJ Griffiths & Cartright. Taken out by Pat Jennings, paid by CF. Paid out to Pat Jennings, female present, probably CF.
6. COR/MJ. & CTTL/TH, J. Smith (only 13 weeks' premiums paid, grant made because of plea of poverty) Paid to CF (aunt) and another woman. Mrs Stanton involved.
7. CTTL/MJ Whithead & COR/MJ Dolan. Taken out by CF, paid out to CF & PJ.
8. CTTL/MH J. Williams. Taken out by and paid out to MH N.B. 11s. 6d. deducted as only 1s. 6d. premium had been paid

John Flanagan (some documents missing relating to these insurances)				
Company	date taken out	amount insured	amount paid	date paid
Prudential Ass. Co.[9]	June 1879	£24 18s.	£24 18s.	? died 7.12.1880
Victoria Legal Friendly Society[10]	Oct. 79	increased to £23 2s.	£15	?
Pearl Ass. Co.[11]	?	£7 16s.	£3 16s.	?
L'pool Protective Burial Soc.[12]	Feb. 1880	£24	£12	?
Wesleyan & General Ass. Co.[13]	3 Sept. 1880	£15 14s.	£15 14s.	?
Totals		£95 10s.	£71 8s.	

9. CTTL/JF, Bond, Gwynne & Marshall. CF paid and claimed.
10. CTTL/JF, Hoolihan, wife proposed, CF encouraged.CF paid after wife's death.
11. CTTL/JF Hivey/JD Bowles.Paid to CF.
12. CTTL/JF, Clarke. Taken out by CF paid out to CF.
13. CTTL/ JF. Griffiths. CF paid, paid out to CF.

Street shop at prices ranging from 20s. to 40s. Top range marble clocks could be obtained for £10 or an alarm clock from 6s. 6d.[5]

Leaving moral condemnation aside, it was a remarkably clever manipulation of burial society rules to use impersonation and blatant lies to perpetrate what amounted to a complicated system of insurance fraud. The women were never given credit, if that be the appropriate term, for having the aptitude and intelligence to achieve that. Illiterate the sisters may have been, but they were clever, far-seeing and had considerable business acumen. The Liverpool Daily Post[6] on 18 February 1884 waxed philosophically (but erroneously) that 'persons in their class of life have little knowledge of the property of poisons and less ability to form a craft scheme of crime.' The two sisters were clever enough to deceive and manipulate the doctors so that they completed the death certificates without question. They were systematically and criminally deceitful to achieve their own ends. That aspect of their characters was underestimated, if not totally ignored, presumably because it would have been rather embarrassing for the literate professionals who had been so utterly duped by them.

Catherine Flanagan is portrayed as forceful and not a woman to be crossed, as shown by the revelations concerning her slander action against Mrs Hoare. She won the action and was awarded compensation, damages and costs.[7] Once again, no 'credit' was given for the blatant audacity of this.[8]

'She was wearing ...'

There are more details available about Catherine Flanagan's appearance, probably because she absconded. The police needed to issue a description of Catherine to aid arrest. She was described in detail, the text of the 'wanted' poster being published in the *Liverpool Echo* on 16 October 1883:[9]

> About 50, 5′ 2″ in height, stout built, full features, fresh complexion, freckled face, dark eyes, dark, wavy hair turning grey. Two teeth out in front of upper jaw, scar from a cut-mark, right side, upper lip, thick lips, cut-mark on left eye-brow, small nose, slightly turned up. Wears large gold earrings and has several rings on her fingers, speaks with a strong Irish accent ... dressed in black dress, black shawl & bonnet.

Of necessity it needed to be accurate or the police would have had an even more difficult task of finding and arresting her. It took them long enough as it was, she was so well protected.

There is great emphasis on what clothes she was wearing, and throughout her flight those who were later to see her or give her shelter gave detailed accounts of not only what she wore, but other clothes she had with her at the time.[10] Even today's court reporters seem unable to omit descriptions of the defendant's clothing, as if a description of T-shirt and jeans assists the reader to establish guilt or innocence.

On arriving at her first place of sanctuary she is said to have worn 'an ordinary striped skirt with a shawl over her head and underneath her arm a bundle containing the black silk dress which she at present wears as well as a stuff jacket and a new black stuff dress.'[11]

This description lacks what might be expected, namely the emphasis on uncleanliness, unkempt appearance or unladylike dress. On one night, it is presumed she had sheltered in an outhouse in the absence of formal lodgings and then her appearance is described in the *Liverpool Echo* on 17 October as 'fatigued'.[12]

On her arrest she was described in the local press[13] as wearing 'a black silk dress which was in good condition and although otherwise respectably dressed she has what might be called a gypsy-like appearance about her.

Throughout her arrest she appeared to be perfectly unconcerned and extremely cool.' They added that she was quite sober. This last comment surely demonstrates a desire for accuracy rather than sensation to please the voyeuristic reader: a drunken prisoner might have been more true to the image of the deviant woman of the Victorian era.

Margaret Higgins comes across less clearly, in the shadow of her sister. Whether this is a deliberate ploy on the part of the press to justify their portrayal of Flanagan as the more dominant of the two, or whether the press had no interest in her as she was safely in prison, unlike her fleeing sister, cannot be ascertained.

There are no references to Margaret Higgins' appearance before her arrest and at the trial she is described almost as an afterthought. During the proceedings the two sisters were depicted sitting in the dock, Flanagan being 'well dressed but Higgins was in a print dress with a shawl over her head.' This appears purely factual without bias in any particular direction.

Even at their execution their clothes did not escape attention. Both sisters were dressed in black and Flanagan wore round her neck a link of rosary beads. Their measurements are coldly and carefully recorded. The *Liverpool Daily Post*[14] reported Flanagan was 4' 11¾" and weighed 113 lb. Her sister was taller, at 5' 3¾" and heavier at 130 lb.

Leaving aside the editorials written after conviction, which are dealt with below, the descriptions as a whole seem to be those of average, working-class, middle-aged women who might be seen in the poorer areas of Liverpool in the 1880s. The fact that they killed could not be deduced simply by reading those details of shawls and dresses. There is no reference to the facial characteristics of Margaret Higgins, and the only details available of Catherine Flanagan, as mentioned above, were of necessity made as accurate as possible for the assistance of the police officers who were looking for her. Indeed, excepting the facial scars, 'fresh complexion, freckled face, dark eyes, dark, wavy hair turning grey, small nose, slightly turned up' is hardly the stuff of nightmares. The conclusion must be that there was no pre-conviction manipulation of their physical image.

'How did they behave ...?'

Because the deviant Victorian woman was allegedly callous, hard and lacking maternal warmth, the expectation is that both sisters would be portrayed as such in the press reports, both before and during the commission of the crimes and at the trial. It is difficult, but nevertheless necessary, to differentiate between opinion and factual accounts of the two women's actions. Thus the evidence of their actions as shown in the chapter on victims hopefully reveals their true characters, which can then be compared with the image put forward in the press reports.

The second difficulty is that it is impossible to ascertain whether witnesses to factual matters are keeping to the absolute truth or whether they are exaggerating, either to boost their own importance in the eyes of their peers, create a sensation in court or, like James MacKenzie, to play down their own nefarious activities. Mr MacKenzie assisted Catherine Flanagan to evade arrest and his evidence given at the Assize Court is examined in detail in the chapter dealing with her flight from the police. Even so, it is probably safe to assume that evidence on oath in an intimidating court arena is more likely to produce a version of events closer to the truth than a statement gathered by a news reporter. At least, the opportunity for challenge is there, and, as in the case of Mr MacKenzie, the chance for the judge to express his disbelief.

While evading arrest, Catherine Flanagan was described by one of her friends (Mrs MacKenzie) [15] as 'half tipsy or stupid and greatly upset', then 'greatly distressed' and walking about all night, unable to sleep. Hardly the description of a hard, callous woman. When later taken in by Mrs Booth her new hostess felt sufficient empathy to generally nurse and 'coddle' her because of rheumatism. This gives the impression of a normal woman in some physical distress, who engaged the sympathy of another, no more no less. She was clearly not ostracised by her peer group, which demonstrates the caring aspect of the community network.[16]

Taking the Victorian image of the deviant woman as a parameter, the reports of the demeanours of the two prisoners during their trial are unexpected. There were no suggestions of hardness or brutality, just a listless sorrow and resignation.[17] The *Liverpool Daily Post* reported on 15 February 1884 that:

> Both listened intently. Flanagan moved restlessly and frequently put her handkerchief to her eyes. Higgins sat nearly motionless leaning back with a weary look on her face as if wishing it was over. Neither of them attempted to communicate with their counsel

and it was not a case in which communication could have been very useful.

When Catherine Flanagan's daughter Ellen appeared, her mother 'dropped her face in her hands and seemed to be almost overcome', surely a fairly reported indication of shame and motherly love.

Margaret Higgins too was credited with some softer feeling, when evidence was give of exhumations. The two local newspapers on 16 February[18] noted that 'Mrs Higgins showed the first sign of emotion which she had exhibited in the trial, she leaned forwards and seemed to be weeping', but the reporter suggested it was only temporary, for he continued, 'but in a few moments she recovered herself and resumed her old attitude of wearied indifference.' It is difficult to know whether the 'indifference' was meant to indicate callousness or resignation to her fate.

'Disgraceful ...!'

Anticipating a very harsh condemnation of the two sisters, the contemporary press reports were surprisingly much more balanced before and during the trial than I had expected. What they were alleged to have done was described in detail (and those details were factually grim) but the reporting is not vitriolic at this stage. The journalists did generally write in a style which tended to be histrionic with liberal use of exciting adjectives such as 'terrible' and 'shocking'. As an example, the headlines on page 4 of the *Liverpool Echo* for Saturday October 13, 1883 include 'Shocking Accident of the Cheshire Lines Railway', 'Heartless Deception', 'Gone Mad in Betting', 'Miss Morphia's Sister', 'The Salvationist Nuisance', and on 6 November 1883: 'Alleged Extraordinary Robbery' and 'Who Killed the Cat, A Tranmere Outrage'.

The majority of reports about the activities of the sisters are grossly prejudicial to a fair trial by today's standards but are not personal to Flanagan or Higgins. They were portrayed not so much as wicked women than as instruments of the greater evils of lax insurance laws and unregistered sales of poisons. The reports mostly concentrated on Flanagan, describing what she did, or was alleged to have done, and suggested her lifestyle tended to be on the wrong side of the law, but they did not condemn her as a woman; the subject could as easily have been a man.

The reports must be read with an appreciation that the press were not as strictly controlled as regards pre-trial reporting as they are now. Thus while Flanagan was being sought by the police her character was adversely criticised in the press in such terms as: 'The antecedents of Mrs Flanagan are said not to have been of a reputable character.' The term 'family clubber' is used and explained in such a way as to leave the reader in no doubt that not only was Mrs Flanagan in the habit of insuring acquaintances in the hope of reaping rewards, but that it was common practice among her neighbours. A more specific allegation was made in the *Liverpool Echo* on 15 October 1883 regarding Mrs Flanagan 'who is suspected of having first entered people in burial clubs and friendly societies and afterwards poisoned them for the insurance money'. Two days later the *Liverpool Echo* confided to its readers[19] that no one had been called to formally identify Mrs Flanagan 'as she is well known to some members of the Force', and the *Liverpool Daily Post*[20] for that day continues, 'particularly by one or two of the detectives who have been following her up lately.'

From 10 October 1883 onwards, the *Liverpool Echo*[21] adopted the headline 'Alleged Wholesale Poisoning' when reference was made to the case, the word 'alleged' sometimes being omitted. On other occasions it is referred to as 'the Liverpool Poisoning mystery'. The *Liverpool Daily Post* tended to refer to the story as 'Alleged Poisoning in Liverpool' or 'Alleged Wholesale Poisoning' or 'The Liverpool Poisoning Case'.

An optimist among the *Liverpool Daily Post* reporters stated on 15 October 1883[22] that the authorities were hoping for an early arrest of the person 'who appears to have been the prime mover' in what they describe as 'a very dirty job'. Again, the blame is put onto the elder of the two sisters, assuming her guilt yet not condemning her specifically as a woman, just as a person. Her flight was regarded as a pointer to her guilt[23] with reports referring to her as one 'who has taken such a sudden and suspicious departure.' Yet it revealed that she still had some friends who sheltered her and hid her, and afterwards, when the coast was clear, said 'Thanks be to God, Mrs Flanagan, ye have luck yet.' This accords with another report:[24] 'According to our information it would appear that a system of terrorism has been exercised by those in sympathy with efforts of the absconding woman to evade arrest.' The newspapers reported this almost as if there was a sneaking admiration for her evasion of the police and the *Liverpool Echo* had reported the previous day, rather resentfully, that[25] her close friends were 'impenetrably silent as to her career and recent habits'.

When news leaked of the new allegation of Maggie Jenning's murder, the *Liverpool Daily Post* on 12 October 1883 predicted[26] that it would 'increase the suspicion that is felt as to Mrs Flanagan's conduct for some years past and add to necessity for thorough investigation of the charges made against her'. An appallingly prejudicial comment appeared in the *Liverpool Echo* on 16 October when it was alleged that Catherine[27] insured people and then poisoned them. In December, the *Liverpool Echo* reported that[28] 'Mrs Flanagan from some reason or other, did not appear to have had an enviable reputation in the locality.'

There are general reports taken from statements given to the reporters by lodgers, neighbours and acquaintances which go some way to build a picture of women who do not live up to the Victorian ideal of loving, caring housewives, but they are not totally condemnatory; the criticisms are, if anything, guarded and slightly oblique. On 11 October 1883 the *Liverpool Echo*[29] featured the statement of Patrick Jennings given to their reporter and contained the quoted warning to him, by a neighbour, of: 'God help you, you poor man, I am sorry for you. Mind yourself while you are there.' The next day the *Liverpool Echo*[30] erroneously stated that Dr Whitford was not sent for until the day before Thomas Higgins died, although there was no specific condemnation of the sisters for lack of care.

CHAPTER 4

Catherine's last days
of freedom

'Ran away! Why should she not?'

Mr Shee, counsel for the defence

WHILE Margaret waited in obscurity in her prison cell, it was
Catherine who drew all the press attention as she took flight and
became a celebrated fugitive.

Many a back door has facilitated a hasty exit and the one at 27 Ascot
Street proved no exception in October 1883. The corpse of Thomas
Higgins lay in the house, awaiting the hearse which was to take him
to his final place of rest. Before the undertaker arrived, however, the
coroner's beadle and Dr William Whitford entered the house to ascertain
the cause of his death. His widow Margaret and her sister, Catherine
Flanagan, knew perfectly well what had prompted his demise and
indeed, had caused other sudden deaths in the vicinity. Their efforts with
arsenic-impregnated flypapers had been very successful in the recent
past but Thomas was their final victim.

Catherine Flanagan's sense of self-preservation propelled her out of
the house on Thursday 4 October 1883, and she managed to remain
out of the hands of the police for the next ten days, moving from one
safe house to another with the help of friends, acquaintances and their
contacts.

The detail of how she achieved this is fascinating and shows how
the community enfolded and protected her, 'closing ranks' against the
persistent questioning of the press reporters and remaining silent and

uncooperative (and in some cases conspiratorially obstructive) in the face of determined investigation and searching by Liverpool police officers.

When the prosecuting counsel, Mr Aspinall, opened the case for the Crown[1] he said he would give the jury the history of her 'proceedings' as it would be very material to the prosecution's case. By hearing where she went and what she said they would be able to see that she was 'alarmed beyond measure by the proceedings which had been taken'. It was certainly her absence rather than her presence which attracted the attention of the press in the aftermath of Thomas Higgins' death.

When Mr Shee, the counsel for the defence, rose to make his closing speech to the jury, he dealt first with the reason why Catherine Flanagan ran away. As he put it, 'Ran away! Why should she not?' and went on to imply that she had been afraid, but nevertheless innocent, before turning his attention to other aspects of the prosecution's case. The press report in the *Liverpool Echo*[2] of his closing speech is little more than a précis and the full excuse for absconding is not pursued. It is not mentioned at all in the *Liverpool Daily Post*'s report[3] but that paper does inform the reader that Mr Shee's speech lasted for one and a half hours.

By referring to the evidence given at the inquest into the death of Thomas Higgins and the later committal proceedings, it is possible to trace her movements, step by step, safe house by safe house. This, as much as any verbal narrative, amply demonstrates how the closed community assisted its own, thwarting the efforts of the police.

Meanwhile her sister languished in police custody, probably being arrested on that Thursday, but certainly in a cell by the next day. This is confirmed by Inspector Edwin Maxwell, who told the coroner: 'I found the prisoner Higgins at the Detective Office on the night of 5 October last.'

Thursday 4 October

According to Patrick Jennings,[4] Catherine Flanagan disappeared from the Ascot Street house on Thursday 4 October 1883 when Patrick Higgins and Dr Whitford arrived at about half past one, but Jennings saw her again about two thirty with Mrs Ryan going towards her own home in Latimer Street. Shortly afterwards he found she had left there.

Later[5] she went to the house of Maria MacKenzie[6] at 4 Rockingham Street (a ten or fifteen minute walk away from Ascot and Latimer

Street[7]), arriving there between five and six p.m. They were acquainted through Mrs MacKenzie's sister, Margaret Parkhouse, who had once lived with Catherine Flanagan (and survived!).

On her arrival, Flanagan was wearing a shawl over her head and had a bundle under her arm which Mrs MacKenzie later discovered contained a silk dress and a black stuff dress. Flanagan had no dress on, it was under her arm, and she was wearing a striped petticoat.

Catherine said she was in great trouble, and running away from her son who had been drinking and was 'after her' for drawing £7 10s. 0d. club money. Mrs MacKenzie described Flanagan as 'very uneasy' all the time she was there. She expanded this to 'half tipsy or stupid and greatly upset' when interviewed by the press.[8] She kept a small sweet shop and she noticed that every time a customer came in Mrs Flanagan would run to the scullery. Mrs MacKenzie was adamant that Flanagan did not mention any deaths to her.

After drinking some tea and staying all evening, Catherine asked if she could remain there that night. Mrs MacKenzie agreed. The *Daily Post*[9] reported Mrs MacKenzie as saying that Flanagan expressed an intention of going to Scotland as her son was in the habit of ill-treating her and she was glad to leave what she had left behind in Latimer Street to him.

Flanagan slept that night in the same bed with Mrs MacKenzie's sister, Margaret Parkhouse. She, on coming home from work, found Mrs Flanagan there and was told by her that Thomas Higgins was dead, Margaret Higgins drunk and Patrick Flanagan was chasing her for the club money. Flanagan went to bed about 8.30 to 9 p.m. but was still awake when Margaret Parkhouse joined her about 10.30. She noticed Flanagan was wearing her petticoat and a flannel nightdress. Margaret seems to have had a disturbed night, her companion sitting at the foot of the bed.'I cannot rest, Maggie' was the only explanation she was given.

Friday 5 October

Margaret Parkhouse went off to work at 6 a.m. the next morning, returning for breakfast at 8.30 to be questioned by Mrs Flanagan about whether she had heard 'anything' at her work. Margaret did not seem to know what she was talking about.

That morning Catherine asked her hostess to fetch her daughter Nelly (Ellen Flanagan) and again expressed her unease and bewilderment, saying 'I don't know whatever it's to do with me'.[10] When giving evidence to the coroner[11] Mrs MacKenzie stated that Flanagan warned her to bring Ellen secretly so that no one would see her come. Ellen was duly brought and Mrs MacKenzie heard her tell her mother, 'My uncle's heart has been taken out and my aunt has been taken up ... The neighbours say you have poisoned my uncle'. Mrs MacKenzie heard Mrs Flanagan explain to Ellen that both her aunt and uncle had been drinking for a full month and all that she was involved in was the club money and that was the reason for her staying away. Mrs MacKenzie was unable to hear the rest of the conversation but did gather that Ellen was given one of her mother's black dresses with instructions to cut it up for herself and told to return next day with all the news. She did, it seems, return for a short time that night but after that did not reappear until Saturday evening. When this is reported in the press[12] there is a slight difference. Mrs MacKenzie there stated that on the first visit Ellen received instructions to get the bonnet and black and white shawl, and on her second visit she referred to the post-mortem, whereupon Mrs Flanagan seemed 'greatly disturbed'.

On Friday evening when Margaret Parkhouse returned from her work at 7 p.m. she found Mrs Flanagan still there, in the rocking chair. There followed an interesting exchange between the two women in which Parkhouse says: 'I was the first to speak. I said I had heard a funeral stopped by a man's wife's sister having poisoned him.' Mrs Flanagan apparently said, 'People will say anything these days', then the subject was dropped. It is surely inconceivable that Margaret Parkhouse did not realise the relevance of the rumour she had passed on. She had formerly lodged with Mrs Flanagan, so would know her family ties. Flanagan had told her the previous day that her sister's husband was dead, there was a problem over the club money and her going into hiding was a consequence. Margaret Parkhouse was now sharing a bed with her and suffering disturbed nights as a result.

James MacKenzie, Maria's husband, returned home from his work at about the same time as his sister-in-law, he too being told by Mrs Flanagan of her troubles with her son and the club money. He said he had not been aware of her presence in the house the previous evening as he had returned home very late that night. He gives the impression of being totally lacking in curiosity, not querying the presence in his home of a woman, whom, he says, he had only known for about two years, and never intimately, and whom he had not seen for months. Either that or he chose not to delve further, fearing that too much knowledge could, for him, be dangerous.

Friday proved to be yet another restless night for Margaret Parkhouse, with Flanagan saying she could not sleep as 'she seen it all before her', and refusing a soothing drink of milk proffered by Margaret.

Saturday 6 October

On Saturday morning, Margaret went to work as usual at 6 a.m. returning for breakfast to face more questioning by Mrs Flanagan. She asked whether she had seen anything on placards. Apparently she had not. She was then asked to fetch a paper and read it to Mrs Flanagan but as Margaret could not read, her sister Mrs MacKenzie acquired a paper and persuaded a neighbour, Mrs Collins to read it, but there was nothing about the topic of funerals being stopped that Mrs Flanagan had been so interested in. Surely the penny would have dropped by now?

Margaret was then asked to fetch Ellen but refused on the grounds that she was going back to work until about 2 p.m. and could not neglect her work. On being offered payment, however, she relented and found Ellen after her work and delivered her mother's message.

It seems that Ellen came to her mother about 4 p.m. that afternoon and although Margaret Parkhouse could not hear the conversation (one assumes she tried) she saw the girl was crying. She later saw Ellen write notes for her mother. On Saturday evening Ellen returned and Mrs Flanagan told her to bring her bonnet and shawl as she was going to Scotland.

Apparantly Ellen left on Saturday evening and then returned to tell her mother (according to Mrs MacKenzie) that the 'the detectives have taken a vinegar bottle and have been smelling all the bottles in Auntie's cellar'. Mrs Flanagan then took a bunch of keys from the market pocket that she was wearing, telling Ellen to 'make away with her winter medicine bottle and her likeness'; she said the bottle was either in her drawer or box and the likeness was over the drawers. (Ellen persistently denied being told anything about a bottle whenever she was questioned in court about it.)

Either Mrs MacKenzie was eavesdropping or the conversation was open in front of her. It is unlikely by this stage that she would not, at the very least, have had some suspicions about Flanagan's presence in her home.

Mrs MacKenzie's child was sent for writing paper, Ellen wrote two notes for her mother (as Margaret Parkhouse said) and took them away.

Mrs MacKenzie told the reporter from the *Post*[13] that Mrs Flanagan went out on that Saturday night 'drinking at "Pearsons"' which tends to throw some credibility on the speculation of the *Post* reporter[14] that Flanagan was 'in the vicinity of Latimer Street on Saturday evening ... well disguised, head enveloped in a thick shawl and walked along, lame, with the use of heavy stick, but she stopped to speak to one or two of her staunch friends in order to become acquainted with the latest efforts of and raids of the authorities to arrest her.' It suggested that she was still hiding in one of the slums between Sylvester Street and Athol Street where she had 'many friends and acquaintances. Indeed we shall not be far wrong if we say that those people in Latimer Street, Martin, Athol Street who know anything at all about Mrs Flanagan are her close friends who are impenetrably silent as to the career and recent habits, most of whom being, also like herself, money lenders in a small way'.

It seems from that comment that the press could not extract any information out of her 'friends' any more than the police could, demonstrating the tight loyalties of the community. This is precisely the same anti-authority and anti-police co-operation as that which Ellen Ross[15] describes in her work on survival networks; a miscreant could be aided in his escape via a fast-opening door, stolen goods hidden while the pursuing police officers were kept talking by a domineering matron.

Margaret Parkhouse (wisely perhaps) spent the rest of the weekend with friends and when she returned home on the next Monday, Flanagan had gone.

Sunday 7 October

Sunday night, Ellen returned with a black bonnet and shawl and gold wedding ring. Mrs Flanagan was then in a black silk dress; she put on the bonnet and shawl, put on the wedding ring and another on top. She then left Mrs MacKenzie, paying her a 2s. piece and promising a 'nice present' when she came back. (Mrs MacKenzie was not to see Mrs Flanagan again until she appeared in court.) She and Ellen left, destination unknown, but on the way, according to Mrs MacKenzie, invited Mr MacKenzie for a drink and he duly went with her.

(When Maria MacKenzie was interviewed by the *Post*[16] she gave a slightly different account of Flanagan's leaving. She says she left on Sunday saying she was going to Scotland and taking her daughter with her. She added, 'while she stayed in this house it was no secret who she was for several of the neighbours knew about it.' It goes without saying then, that nobody thought to tell the authorities.)

James MacKenzie, Mrs Flanagan and Ellen went, at Flanagan's request, to a house in Jordan Street, not for a drink as Mrs MacKenzie said, but to avoid the possibility of Flanagan's son coming to the MacKenzie household and annoying them. The three of them walked to Smith Street, which is off Stanley Road, and then Mrs Flanagan hired a cab. Ellen left them at this stage. The cab drove them to Cornwallis Street where Mrs Flanagan then said that she could not recall where her friends, with whom she had been intending to seek lodgings, lived. MacKenzie then took her to Blundell Street (he hardly knew her, remember) to his friend Barrett to see if he could recommend lodgings, having first met Barrett's aunt, Sarah Daley.

Then Barrett, his aunt, Flanagan and MacKenzie went to a public house and had a drink. This does give the impression that there was an impregnable circle of safety which allowed Flanagan to move about freely without being apprehended by the police. It is not every fugitive who feels sufficiently secure to take the aunt of an acquaintance out for a drink. After two or three abortive attempts to find lodgings, the four went to 49 Lydia Anne Street where Mrs Flanagan was accepted as a lodger by Mrs Burns. Mr MacKenzie later adopted a staunch, upright, law-abiding citizen mode when appearing before the coroner, and as he described the moment when they arranged the lodgings added, 'more's the pity we did'.

During James MacKenzie's evidence at the trial it was at this point in the story that the judge, Mr Justice Butt, interrupted.[17] 'His Lordship here remarked that if the story of the witness and his wife were correct it did not do them credit. They had heard that the doctor had taken the heart and liver out of the man Higgins [In all fairness they heard Ellen refer to heart, not liver] and that Flanagan had poisoned the deceased [Ellen only told her mother that the neighbours were spreading rumours about poison] and yet they did not make any enquiries. If it did not look very much like getting them out of the way he did not know what did.' The court was left in no doubt as to the judge's view of Mr MacKenzie's credibility.

Mrs Margaret Burns gave evidence that she first met Mrs Flanagan on that night of Sunday 7 October. She was brought to her house by Barrett and MacKenzie. The two men had apparently asked about the room and accepted it before Mrs Flanagan set foot on the doorstep. There was another woman with them at the time; accounts differ, but it was either Barrett's aunt or Mrs Burns' daughter[18] who had been accosted by Barrett, MacKenzie and Flanagan in their quest for lodgings.

Mrs Burns told the jury[19] that 'MacKenzie told me she was a friend off the Irish boat', and she also told the Daily Post reporter, 'One of the men said that the woman had come off the Irish boat and that she would pay a week in advance if she could get lodgings.'[20] (MacKenzie knew full well that was not true and Barrett had never met Mrs Flanagan before in his life, so whichever man said it, it shows deception.) Mrs Flanagan went along with that story, calling herself Mrs McCormack. This surname (sometimes spelt McCormick) appears interwoven with the Flanagan family. There is a family named McCormack in the same house in Blenheim Street as Catherine Flanagan at the time of the 1881 census, and Margaret Parkhouse, sister of Mrs MacKenzie, lived in Hornby Street with a Mrs McCormick at the time of the trial. Catherine Flanagan also said her son, who went to prison, was called John McCormack. It is this name which fuels suspicion that Catherine may have been married to a Mr McCormack before John Flanagan, but it cannot be taken further.

The new lodger duly sent for and paid for some beer, which they all drank, and then 'Mary McCormack'[21] was left in the care of Mrs Burns where she stayed until the following Tuesday, never once leaving the premises.

As Mrs Burns later anonymously told the reporter from the Daily Post:[22]

She did not stir out of the house from the night she set foot in my house until Tuesday evening. At about four o'clock on Tuesday afternoon she asked me if the evening papers came up that way, and I said, 'They do sometimes.' She then gave me a penny and asked me to go out for an Echo. I brought an Echo back with me and she requested me to see if John McCormack had been tried that day. I took John McCormack to be her son so I put on my spectacles and looked over the paper but could see nothing of the trial she had mentioned. As I was glancing at the *Echo* however something attracted my attention and I said 'Oh, dear me!' 'What is it?' she said and I replied, 'It is the Wholesale Poisoning Case.'[23]

She then asked me to read it for her and I did so, but when I had finished I exclaimed 'Oh, the walking devil!' meaning Mrs Flanagan, 'I could find it in my heart to string her up myself.' She replied, 'Oh, she's a bad 'un' and afterwards walked away from me. Between half past eight o'clock and nine the same night the same two men who had brought Mrs Flanagan to my house came for her. One of them said, 'Hurry up and put your bonnet and shawl on, I want to speak to you outside.' I asked them to go upstairs into the parlour to speak and they did so. They had not been up long before she came down and said 'Oh, he's gone.' I asked her who she meant and she said 'My son,' and I, thinking that she meant he was dead, answered 'God help you.' She afterwards said that he was in prison and that she would have to go to him. Shortly afterwards she left with the two men and went in the direction of Kent Street. When she was going I invited her to come and see me again, but if I had known who she was I would have seen her and her half crown at the bottom of the sea.

Mrs Burns seems to have been completely taken in by Mrs Flanagan and misled by the two men who brought her.

Tuesday 9 October

The events of Tuesday 9 October show that both Barrett and MacKenzie were beginning to fear for their own safety. Their two versions of events differ slightly in detail. Both men said they 'heard things' independently and began to suspect Catherine Flanagan's motives so they met and discussed the matter.

Barrett, who was literate, told the coroner that on the Tuesday (9 October) he read about the poisoning case in the paper, went to Mrs Burns' house and accused Flanagan of being Mrs Flanagan from the north end, Latimer Street. She denied it, so he did not pursue matters and accepted what she said. Nevertheless he retained some suspicion; as he said, he knew she had come from the north end with Mr MacKenzie yet had heard her tell Mrs Burns she had come on the Irish boat on

Sunday morning. When he saw James MacKenzie later, they discussed it and went to see her at the Burns house as MacKenzie described.

According to MacKenzie's later version of events, on Tuesday 9 October he heard 'something at the docks' so when he later met Barrett they went to 49 Lydia Anne Street. Barrett's version of events approximates with MacKenzie's with minor variations. MacKenzie said he went into the house, and said to Flanagan.'You have brought me into a nice disgrace ... you are blamed for poisoning Mr Higgins.' He then told her to put on her bonnet and shawl and come outside. She did so but persuaded them to go to a public house rather than stand in the street. He said he challenged her about what he had heard of the news report but she called him foolish and denied it, laughing it off. He says he did not persist in the questioning.

After drinking they left the public house an hour later and went to another, Mrs Flanagan paying all the time. Barrett then left them.

MacKenzie says he asked several times what she was going to do with herself, 'go home or give yourself up?'[24] but she told him to mind his own business. In his evidence to the coroner he said he asked her bluntly: 'Have you done this deed?' and received the response, 'No, go away.'

So he did.

There is no record of what Mrs Flanagan did after that exchange, but it is likely that she spent the night sleeping rough. According to the *Daily Post*,[25] 'from her fatigued appearance next morning she is supposed to have taken shelter in some outhouse.'

Despite the *Post*'s inclination towards a more sensational style of reporting than that of the *Echo*, an interesting nuance is reported and it is worthwhile scrutinising the part played by Barrett and MacKenzie in Catherine's flight.

According to the report in the *Daily Post*,[26] after leaving Mrs MacKenzie in Rockingham Street Mrs Flanagan went to Lydia Anne Street. It propounded the theory that the plan was to go from house to house to evade detection by the police: 'Timely warning also appears to have been given the prisoner when to make her next move and the two men already referred to in our introduction were seen about with her in one or two neighbourhoods assisting her evidently in her endeavours to move out of town'. The introduction referred to reads: 'It is not unlikely that in the course of a day or two other persons may be arrested and charged, if not with being concerned in the alleged murder, at all events with being accessory to it after the fact.'

If indeed the police were thinking along those lines it is no wonder that MacKenzie gave his evidence as he did.

Thomas Barrett remains a shadowy figure, as little is known about him.[27] According to the *Liverpool Echo* of 15 December 1883, he is a labourer living at 35 Blundell Street. This is adjacent to Cornwallis Street where the MacKenzies lived. The only trace of a Thomas Barrett in Liverpool in the 1881 census surname index for Lancashire is a 24-year-old bachelor, occupation dock labourer, the same as James MacKenzie. It seems likely that this was the right man.

He was a stranger to Mrs Flanagan and first met her on the Sunday night of 7 October when she was with his aunt (Sarah Daley). They all went for a drink in a public house in St James' Street. Barrett was approached by Mr MacKenzie who said he needed lodgings for someone for one or two nights, perhaps up to a week. Barrett took them to 49 Lydia Anne Street, the home of Mrs Burns.

According to the press,[28] Flanagan and two men asked a young woman in Kent Street if she could recommend lodgings; that woman turned out to be Mrs Burns' daughter and she led them to her mother's house.

Whatever the sequence, Mrs Burns was then faced with Mrs Flanagan who, she told the *Post* reporter,[29] called herself Mary McCormack.

When giving evidence at the committal proceedings, Barrett told the court: 'Mrs Flanagan said to Mrs Burns her name was Mrs McCormack'. James MacKenzie was apparently there at the time yet did not contradict her. Barrett then left Mrs Flanagan and James MacKenzie with Mrs Burns. He later told the coroner, 'Mr MacKenzie spoke of Mrs Flanagan as Bridget but she introduced herself as Mrs McCormack.' His evidence at the trial differed slightly,[30] in that he said 'she gave the name of Bridget McCormack' and he heard MacKenzie call her by that name.

Barrett too waited until Flanagan was arrested before going to the police, not realising until then who she was (he said). If he had known, he said, he would have told the police but it did not occur to him. Barrett told the coroner that 'MacKenzie, when I met him at the north end, said he was in trouble and must get the woman out of the Burns house for fear of disgracing it.' He specifically told the committal court that he heard Mr MacKenzie call her Bridget but it was Flanagan herself who introduced herself to Mrs Burns as Mrs McCormack.

Wednesday 10 October

The next morning, Mrs Flanagan went to 3 Mount Vernon Street arriving there about 11.30, attracted by a card in the window. Calling herself Clifford, her maiden name, she enquired of the occupier, Mrs Booth,[31] whether she could stay. Mrs Booth told her she preferred gentlemen lodgers but Mrs Flanagan pleaded, saying she had been travelling all night and had left her luggage on the train. She said she was going to America. Mrs Booth, seeking a reference, was disinclined to accept Mrs Flanagan but soothed by the offer of a sovereign for security and agreed to take her for a week at 4s. per week. Mrs Flanagan promptly went to bed and did not emerge until about 9 a.m. the next morning, Thursday 11 October.

Her new story was that she had come from Manchester to see her niece confined in the Liverpool Workhouse. Mrs Booth challenged her previous story about having travelled all night and received an excuse about being too ashamed to admit the truth.

She stayed in the Booth household until the following Saturday, never going out at all. Mrs Booth told the reporter from the *Daily Post*[32] that Flanagan's excuse was 'rheumatism' so she nursed her generally, in her own words, 'coddled her'. Newspapers were read to her, particularly the articles about the 'Wholesale Poisoning Case' but as a choice of Mrs Booth rather than Mrs Flanagan.

Saturday 13 October

On Saturday 13 October the *Liverpool Echo*[33] reported that police were still making 'vigorous efforts' to arrest Flanagan.'She is known to be in possession of ample means to get out of the country and may consequently baffle the police', it said, but all exits from Liverpool were being covered and the reporter thought she was probably hiding 'in some of the densely populated Irish quarter of the town'. By Monday 15 October[34] the *Echo* rumoured that she was thought to be 'hiding in one of the slums ... between Sylvester Street and Athol Street'. That day's paper also[35] reported a rumour of Catherine's body being found floating near Seacombe Slip. Clearly the press, unable to find facts, were keeping interest alive by exercising their reporter's imagination.

That Saturday's edition of the *Liverpool Echo*[36] carried a report that the day before Flanagan had been hiding in a house over a coalyard in St Martin Street. This is unlikely, bearing in mind Mrs Booth's assertion

that she never left her house, and that same article contains a number
of inaccuracies.[37] For example it says her husband left her and went to
America, and it refers to Catherine as the mother of Margaret Higgins,
whereas they were sisters. It also states that Thomas and Margaret
Higgins were married nine years previously whereas they had been
married less than a year.

The reporter probably picked up the connection between Flanagan
and Ryan and expanded the story. Having accepted that, it does have
some credibility and the incident may well have occurred earlier in
Catherine's flight.

On that Saturday when talk between Mr and Mrs Booth and Mrs
Flanagan turned to the case again, she asked Mr Booth if he thought
Mrs Flanagan would be caught and hanged. He replied in the affirmative.
Only at the trial[38] does Mrs Booth say Flanagan called herself Clifford.
This was clearly a family name, her uncle in Scotland being Thomas
Clifford.[39] Looking at the press reports, the *Liverpool Echo*[40] carried a
report of the resumed inquest into the death of Thomas Higgins. Also
in that paper there was an announcement of the death of Mrs Marwood,
the widow of the late common hangman, together with a separate
article about Marwood's successor. If this was drawn to Mrs Flanagan's
attention it is not likely to have calmed her nerves.'Bartholomew Binns,
the newly appointed public hangman, visited Horncastle yesterday for
the purpose of purchasing the ropes and other apparatus belonging to
the late William Marwood ... When told the ropes and straps had been
sold, he expressed regret.'

Monday 15 October

Flanagan left the house on Monday morning about half past ten saying
she was going to visit her niece. Mrs Booth remarked that she could not
get Mrs Flanagan to eat much at all; she complained of being 'poorly.'
It may well have been Mr Booth's prediction[41] that Flanagan would be
hanged by 'Marwood's successor' that put her off her food.

By 11.15 on that Monday morning, 15 October, Mrs Flanagan reached
Wellington Road in Wavertree and was seen by Mrs Mary McGovern who
was sitting outside her house at 35 Ono Street, knitting. She saw Flanagan
walking backwards and forwards and was eventually asked which station
she was near. Mrs McGovern told her it was Wavertree. Flanagan then
made enquiries about the next station to Blackburn and asked if she could

go inside as she was so tired and offered to pay for a cup of tea. She said there was a warrant out for her. Mrs McGovern kindly refused payment, took her in and gave her tea. They then, with two other women, had ale and Mrs McGovern went and enquired about the trains.

She told Mrs Flanagan that the next train to Blackburn left from Edge Hill at a quarter past twelve and she would have to hurry. As she left the house she threw a bundle under the stairs which turned out to be a jacket. Having missed the first train, Flanagan then returned and for some reason Mrs McGovern read aloud an article in the paper, about the poisoning case. Catherine Flanagan crossed her forehead and said, 'Oh, by the Cross of Christ she was a wicked woman to do such a thing.' This small quotation epitomises the way phrases can mean different things if incorrectly reported. In the press report[42] the inverted commas are inclusive of the whole phrase, whereas in the clerk's notes at the coroner's court[43] it reads as if Mrs Flanagan only says, 'Oh, by the Cross of Christ', and that Mrs McGovern was criticising Mrs Flanagan for making the sign of the cross. One might take a different view of Mrs Flanagan depending on which quotation is correct.

McGovern's daughter, Catherine Ward, showed Flanagan the way to the station but she just missed the train. Ward advised Flanagan she could wait at the Tunnel Hotel for the next train, then Flanagan was approached by a young man with a cart (who was, by this description probably her son Patrick). They spoke, and then all three went for a drink; once again, Mrs Flanagan paid. She had by this time apparently changed her mind about catching the train. She gave her name during this incident as Clifford.

Something jogged Mrs Ward's memory at this point, she later told the coroner and the committal court. She contacted the police, who came to her house, but by then Flanagan had already been taken away by another officer.

Meanwhile, her mother, too, claimed to have had some suspicions.[44] She told a reporter that Flanagan's indiscreet talk about a warrant being out against her for stealing her son's furniture, and the fact that she was showing gold and spending money freely, became talked about and ultimately reached the ears of Inspector Keighley in the police station. He went to the house, apparently more out of curiosity than expectation, and on realising her likeness to the description on the warrant made, one assumes, the arrest of his career. The £5 reward offered by the Head

Constable may have gone to him, but the *Liverpool Daily Post* could not say at that stage.

These two women, mother and daughter, were being kind to a stranger in some distress. Perhaps there was a common bonding of women. They owed her no loyalty once they knew who she was, but one wonders how far they were telling the truth. For example Mrs McGovern does not say that Catherine Flanagan was having dinner with her when she was arrested, as Inspector Keighley attested. Perhaps Mrs McGovern's conscience was troubling her when she gave evidence at the coroner's inquest into Thomas Higgins' death and she resorted to alcohol to steady her nerves. According to the *Liverpool Echo*[45] the coroner, Mr Clarke Aspinall,[46] 'experienced considerable difficulty in getting the witness to answer the questions in a regular manner, and was obliged to caution her that if she did not behave herself she would be sent down to the bridewell. It would be a grievous scandal for a person to come into court in a state of partial intoxication and especially in a case of such solemn importance.' Mrs McGovern answered that she had only had one glass of beer that morning. Her signature on the coroner's deposition is certainly penned with considerably more of a flourish than the one appended to her statement previously taken at the committal proceedings.

Liverpool City Coroner, Mr Clarke Aspinall.

When she had concluded her evidence the press report continues that 'Mr Aspinall spoke kindly to her telling her in future to avoid taking spirits. The witness thanked him and said she would follow his advice.'

Clarke Aspinall was a solicitor and Liverpool City Coroner. He is listed in the 1881 census as aged 53, born Liverpool, living at Laurel Bank, Bebington. He was the brother of John Bridge Aspinall, QC, the Recorder of Liverpool who prosecuted at the trial (nothing like keeping things in the family!).

When opening the case for the prosecution at the trial,[47] Mr John Aspinall, QC, indicated that he would give the jury the details of Flanagan's flight because 'that history would be very material to the case and though the circumstances and conversation might seem when taken singly, yet it was his duty to give them a picture of her proceedings during that time from which he would ask them to infer that during the time she was hiding from justice she was alarmed beyond measure by the proceedings which had been taken. He would ask them to judge that with the rest of the details of the case. But she went from house to house sleeping first in one house and then another on one or two occasions with people she knew and on other occasions almost beseeching for accommodation in houses where she was not known doing one thing and another to which he would call their attention in the aggregate'.

The judge probably had some reservations about this evidence but kept them to himself not realising how protracted the evidence was going to be. The prosecution had ploughed through the various sequences of hosts and hostesses until he reached the evidence pertaining to the Booths' house on Monday before the judge interrupted.[48] He said he did not see how that evidence carried the case further and it seemed to him they were not advancing the case. Mr Aspinall, however, persuaded him otherwise and was allowed to continue.

When Catherine Flanagan was eventually arrested many column inches in both the Echo[49] and the Daily Post were devoted to the 'clever capture by Wavertree Police'[50] (lucky might be a more appropriate adjective).

It seems[51] that Inspector Keighley went first to the Station Hotel, Wellington Road, but on arrival found the suspect had gone to 35 Ono Road, the McGovern House. There he found Mrs Flanagan and the McGoverns having dinner. After questioning her he noticed that her description tallied with that on the handbill in his possession which

Sketch from the *Illustrated Police News*.

gave a detailed description of Catherine Flanagan. He asked if she was indeed the wanted woman but she retorted 'quite coolly and not in the slightest way confused' that she was not. Nevertheless, he arrested her. The inspector noticed that the only difference in her clothing to that described on the bill was that her shawl was black and white instead of black. After her arrest, the paper notes that she replied, 'I know nothing about it,' still retaining her self-possession.

Catherine Flanagan had evaded capture for ten days. It is clear that the majority of people who helped her knew her and probably knew why she was running away.

It is worthwhile looking closely at the carefully contrived evidence of Barrett and MacKenzie and comparing their slightly different versions of their part in the escape. It reinforces the way the closed community assisted its own, thwarting the efforts of the police. James MacKenzie, at the inquest into the death of Thomas Higgins, said he volunteered to tell what he knew at the police station and they told him he would be sent for when wanted. He recollects that this was the day after Flanagan was arrested. He told the coroner he did not go earlier because he was afraid and did not know what to do for the best (best for him, one assumes). He told the jury[52] 'he did not know how to go about it.' It does not take much imagination to picture the expression on the judge's face at this point.

Despite Mr MacKenzie's protestations on oath, it seems likely that he and others went to great length to protect Mrs Flanagan, at potential risk to themselves. Only when she was arrested and beyond help did he abandon her and resort to forgetfulness for his own survival. He says on oath to both the coroner and at the committal that he 'does not remember' calling Mrs Flanagan 'Bridget' as Barrett states; nor 'remember'[53] introducing her to Mrs Burns as Bridget as he 'did not know her Christian name'. Then he added more positively, 'I did not introduce her as Bridget McCormack.'[54]

The press give the impression that Catherine Flanagan was effectively shielded and sheltered not only by friends and acquaintances living within her own community but also by other families, strangers, outside her familiar territory. The police could not penetrate this network and neither could the press. When she was arrested it seems that it was by luck rather than judgement and one only wonders why she was not able to get out of the city quicker.

CHAPTER 5

⟡⟐⟡⟐⟡

Courtroom and scaffold

How many their victims were and when they began their
villainous trade will probably never be known.

Liverpool Daily Post

WHEN Flanagan was arrested, the *Liverpool Echo*, on 19 October,[1] reported that a crowd collected and hooted at her, calling her 'Poisoner, Villain & numerous other epithets.' This report clearly demonstrates peer condemnation, with guilt already determined, but no worse than that, and somewhat milder than the show of animosity that we see nowadays when certain prisoners are arrested and driven to court.

On the same day the *Liverpool Echo*[2] devoted several columns headed 'Mrs Flanagan's Undertaker'. This consisted of a diatribe of vitriol poured liberally onto the reporter's notebook by undertaker Maria Hoare. One of the relatively harmless allegations was that Mrs Flanagan was caught selling beer without a licence and fined for it once or twice. It then continues with a damning indictment of Mrs Flanagan's poisonous activities, such as would halt a trial nowadays. Not all allegations were confined to those which the jury would hear in the months to come including that made by Mrs Hoare that Catherine Flanagan had tried to poison her. She added that there was a great deal of talk and shouting in the street when Mary Donnelly died, accusations of poisoning being made. Little wonder that Flanagan's solicitor Mr Neale wrote a letter to the *Liverpool Echo* complaining about the statement and mentioned the matter, in vain, to stipendiary magistrate Mr Raffles at the committal proceedings.

Some comment should be made about the legal proceedings. The inquests into the first four victims' deaths were conducted by the Coroner of the City of Liverpool, Mr Clarke Aspinall. Each death was dealt with separately over a period of several days and many witnesses were called. All the depositions recorded have survived and are a testament to the care with which the investigations were pursued. The sisters' interests were protected by Mr Henry Fitzwilliam Neale, a 30-year-old Liverpool solicitor. He was joined in his watching brief at the inquests by Mr William Marks, the prosecuting solicitor for Liverpool who undertook the prosecution of the two women in the subsequent proceedings. Mr Quelch, another Liverpool solicitor who had acted for Mrs Hoare in her defence of Flanagan's slander action in 1881, was instructed by Patrick Higgins and appeared on a watching brief on his behalf.

After the inquests, the first stage in the criminal prosecutions took place, with both sisters being charged with all four murders. These were the committal proceedings which took place at the Police Court in Dale Street before Mr Thomas Raffles. Like the Aspinalls, he came from a prestigious Lancashire family and resided at 13 Abercrombie Square, Liverpool.

Mr Neale again defended the sisters as best he could, cross-examining

Abercrombie Square.

the witnesses to best advantage. Here again the clerks' meticulous recording of all the witness statements has been preserved and the questioning and answers are virtually identical to the evidence given at the inquests. Mr Marks prosecuted, his task being infinitely easier than that of Mr Neale.

Both sisters were committed for trial for the murders of Thomas Higgins, Maggie Jennings and John Flanagan junior. Only Margaret Higgins was committed for the murder of her step-daughter Mary Higgins. The stipendiary magistrate found there was insufficient evidence upon which Catherine would be tried on that charge and noted the committal papers accordingly.

THE TRIAL

As was the custom at that time the trial was confined to one charge, the murder of Thomas Higgins. Evidence of the other three deaths was mentioned by way of similar fact evidence.

The trial started on 14 February 1884 at St George's Hall, Liverpool. Mr Justice Butt presided. Sir Charles Parker Butt was born in 1830 and called to the Bar in 1854. He took silk in 1868 and was elected Bencher of Lincoln's Inn in 1869. Between 1880 and 1883 he was the MP for Southampton. In March 1883 he was made a Justice of the High Court, Probate, Divorce and Admiralty Division, and knighted the following month. He died at Wiesbaden in May 1892.

As I have already mentioned the prosecution was represented by Mr John Bridge Aspinall, QC. His junior was William Robert McConnell. Born on 2 July 1837 in Ireland, County Down, he was called to the Bar (Inner Temple) in 1862 and practised on the Northern Circuit. He became Revising Barrister for Liverpool in 1868, and in 1896 he was appointed Chairman of County of London Sessions and took silk. He was held in high regard by his contemporaries for his great ability as a criminal lawyer and was later involved in Florence Maybrick's trial, again as junior to the prosecution.

On their side, the sisters had the services of two very able barristers, appointed before the trial by the presiding judge.

William Pickford was born in 1848 in Rusholme, Lancashire. He was listed in the 1881 census for Liverpool at 101 Bedford Street aged 32. This was just around the corner from Abercrombie Square where Mr Raffles

THE LATE SIR CHARLES PARKER BUTT

Sir Charles Butt, the President of the Admiralty and Divorce Division, who died at Wiesbaden last week, was called to the Bar in 1854. It is perhaps not generally known that, in the early and briefless days of his profession, he devoted himself to journalism, acting as special correspondent of *The Times* at Constantinople. He soon returned to England, however, and after a hard struggle won a name in the Admiralty Court. He took silk in 1868, fourteen years after entering at the Bar. Next year he was elected a Bencher of Lincoln's Inn, and for fourteen years afterwards occupied himself entirely with Admiralty Practice, becoming the recognised leader of the Admiralty Bar. In 1880 he was returned member of Parliament for Southampton, a seat which he retained only for three years, resigning it on his elevation to the Bench as a puisne judge on the death of Sir Robert Phillimore. In 1884 Sir Charles Butt,

THE LATE SIR CHARLES PARKER BUTT
President of the Probate, Divorce, and Admiralty Division
died at Wiesbaden, May 26, 1892

who had meanwhile received the honour of knighthood, served as Royal Commissioner on Merchant Shipping, and much of the recent shipping legislation was largely due to his initiative. In 1891, on the elevation of Sir James Hannen to the peerage, Sir Charles Butt was, with the hearty approval of the profession, appointed President of the Probate, Divorce, and Admiralty Division, and sworn of the Privy Council.

Illustration from *The Graphic,* 4 June 1892.

McConnell, as sketched in *Pall Mall*
Budget, 8 August 1889, p. 997.

Pickford, as sketched in *Pall Mall*
Budget, 8 August 1889, p. 997.

lived. He later defended Florence Maybrick as junior counsel. In due course he became the Recorder for Liverpool and eventually became Master of the Rolls as Lord Sterndale. He died in 1923.

Standing alongside him to defend the sisters was Henry Gordon Shee, born in London in 1847, the second son of Mr Justice Shee. He was called to the Bar at Inner Temple on 30 April 1870, joining the Northern Circuit. The 1881 census lists him in a hotel in Lancashire aged 34, obviously then on circuit with other counsel. He took silk in 1892 and was appointed Recorder of Burnley in 1893. In 1907 he was appointed Recorder of Liverpool replacing William Pickford who was promoted to the High Court. He died on 13 February 1909 in London.

Mr Aspinall opened for the prosecution on the first day of the trial and, after all the evidence had been called, closed his case in a speech which lasted for approximately one hour. Mr Shee's final speech to the jury took one and a half hours and as the newspaper reported, concluded 'with a passionate entreaty the jury to disregard clamour and prejudice and vindicate the impartiality of British Justice' and commented, '... and when Mr Shee sat down it was felt that everything which eloquence learning and ability could do for the prisoners had been most thoroughly accomplished.'

The judge bettered both those learned advocates by addressing the jury in his summing up for two and a half hours. He concluded just before 5 o'clock on Saturday afternoon. The jury filed out to consider their verdict. Three quarters of an hour later they returned with the inevitable one of 'guilty'.

Once the trial began there was a subtle change in the reporting. The excitement of the chase was over, guilt had already been determined by the masses and it was now for the court to formalise the verdict. Apart from a few occasions where the *Liverpool Daily Post* reported incidental scenes in the courtroom, the reporters changed to a more formal style as if determined to be stiff and precise, abandoning conjecture and opinion but still maintaining the intense interest. One moment of mirth (no doubt leaving the two sisters unamused) was reported in the *Liverpool Daily Post* on 16 February.[3] Apparently the trial was interrupted because the attention of all and sundry was diverted by the sight of a 'stout gentleman' who had tried to move from his seat at the back of the court 'but in trying to move past another man of similar proportions he became tightly wedged and could not move for some time', thus proving how crowded the courtroom was.

Reports of the Trial

The *Liverpool Echo* covered the first day of the trial at St George's Hall[4] reporting that the court was not as full as expected.'The sheriff's and the grand jury boxes were almost empty when the judge took his seat upon the bench though the back of the court was very full, but as the day wore on all the available seats were taken up.' The *Liverpool Daily Post*[5] however, offered a different perception under the headline 'Exciting Scenes outside the Court' and told of the huge crowd that had assembled early in the morning with a view to gaining admission to the trial. It reported that 'the court was filled almost as soon as the doors were opened' and 'many thousands had to be turned away'. The excited crowds, according to the *Liverpool Daily Post*, lingered all day and the paragraph continued in almost biblical terms that 'The unanimous opinion amongst the multitude' outside St George's Hall 'was that the women were Guilty and they ought to be hanged, and had they been able to make their appearance as acquitted personages they would in all likelihood have met with the fate of Foulon in the streets of Paris during the Revolution if not that of Horse thieves in Texas, a lamppost being used instead of a tree'. It also reports that they were 'denounced in neither choice language nor measured terms'. It stated that at the end of the day's proceedings the sisters were not transported back to prison in the ordinary prison van, but:

> ... an endeavour was made to get them away quietly in a cab in which they were accompanied by a detective and a police constable. They were recognized however, and a wild yell of hooting raised, which was heard above the roar of the street traffic as far as Monument Place in one direction and Williamson Square in another. A rush was made at the conveyance which was frustrated partly by the activity of police on duty in the neighbourhood and partly by the energy of the driver who lashed his horse into a furious speed and got off amidst the shrieking execrations of the onlookers. No doubt care will be taken this evening to provide the unhappy women with a sufficient escort unless they can be removed from St George's Hall without the knowledge of the crowd.

This is a clear indication of peer condemnation, starkly contrasting with Catherine Flanagan's previous experience of protection and shelter prior to her arrest.

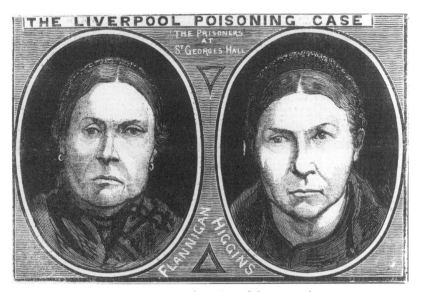

A contemporary depiction of the accused.

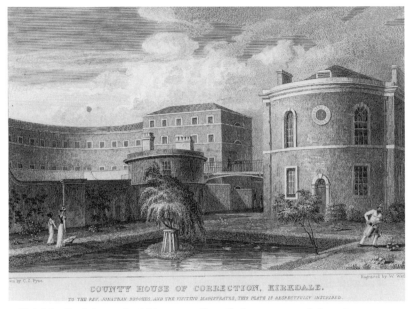

COUNTY HOUSE OF CORRECTION, KIRKDALE.
TO THE REV. JONATHAN BROOKES, AND THE VISITING MAGISTRATES, THIS PLATE IS RESPECTFULLY INSCRIBED.

Kirkdale Gaol, located within two miles of where many of the crimes were committed.

There is a presumption of guilt which pervades all courtroom descriptions.[6] The *Liverpool Echo* confided that when Mr Shee cross-examined chemist Dr Campbell Brown there was 'much sympathy felt for the learned counsel who was so gallantly fighting an uphill battle for a desperate cause'. Women formed over half the audience in the courtroom, as the *Liverpool Daily Post* noted.[7]

Although entitled to legal representation in court, in Victorian England defendants were not entitled to give evidence themselves. Neither of the women, therefore, took the stand.

THE EXECUTIONS

The executions were reported in the press[8] in excruciating detail. The sisters are referred to as 'The wretched women' who were 'quite resigned to their fate' having received Holy Communion the day before their execution and indeed on the morning itself. The papers report that both sisters 'appeared to feel their dreadful position most acutely especially Higgins who since her conviction has evinced much more concern

about her horrible fate than her sister.' Readers were reminded that Mrs
Flanagan tried to secure clemency by giving evidence against her sister,
this being refused. Mrs Higgins, it was said, admitted assisting her
sister in poisoning the victims, and persisted in her claim that she was
acting under the influence of Mrs Flanagan. However, there is no written
evidence to that effect, nor any confirmation in any of the documents
preserved with the Home Office file that supports that contention.

The reporter sets the scene in grotesque detail; snow falling like
a shroud over the area with accompanying piercing chill. It is not a
celebration of death, more a solemn lamentation for evil perpetrated
with an equally evil retribution to follow:

> No feeling of compassion or sympathy could possibly arise for the
> two wretches who were in a few minutes to give their lives as a
> miserable atonement for the many innocent victims whose blood
> they almost battened upon. The thought that these women had
> sent their nearest kith and kin into untimely graves after slow
> agonies of torture by poisoning should, perhaps, have enabled
> the most sensitive heart to regard their richly deserved fate with
> indifference. But no consideration of circumstances could dispel
> the awful sense of dread, which the sight of two women being
> quietly strangled in a courtyard imposed on everyone who had to
> watch the horrible scene.

The *Liverpool Echo*[9] adds: 'Flanagan leaned heavily against Father Bonte
and a warder and repeated the prayers for the dying ... She was ghastly
pale and her eyes were apparently closed.' After prayers the two sisters
'clung to the warders for support and slowly and with effort ascended
the cruel flight of steps'. The phrase 'clung to the warders' seems at
odds with the fact stated further down the page that the sisters' arms
had been securely strapped to their sides before they came out into the
courtyard. No doubt it added to the drama. There is explicit criticism
of the slum dwellers who attended the hanging and waited outside in
the snow, hearing and seeing nothing, yet imagining it all. (It was, it
appears, acceptable for literate upper-class people to read about it in
the newspaper.)

Looking at *The Times*'[10] reporting of the execution of Timothy McVeigh
on 12 June 2001, nothing has changed in 120 years. *The Times* on 4
March 1884[11] devoted only thirty-two lines to the 'Double Execution'

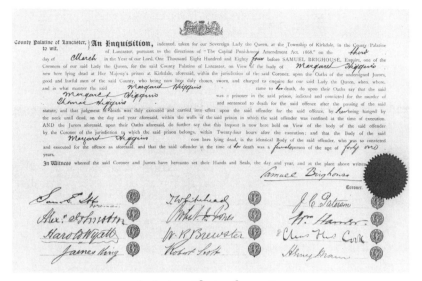

Higgins' certificate of execution.

report, rehearsing the demeanours of the two sisters, but employing much the same tone as the *Echo* reporter.

The report noted that, while 'ghastly pale, Flanagan required little assistance to reach the scaffold', whereas Higgins seemed to have great difficulty 'bearing up under the ordeal', and was supported up the steps to the scaffold by Heath (the executioner's assistant) and a female warder. Higgins, they say, 'seemed to be too much terrified to give heed to the words of Father Bontet' [*sic*] but he 'was calmly listened to by the other culprit'.

The *Liverpool Daily Post* and the *Echo*[12] both reported with identical wording: 'The usual verdict that death had been caused by strangulation was then returned'. *The Times* also gives a brief but different, and more likely, account of the inquest verdict: 'Death was caused by the dislocation of the vertebrae. A verdict in accordance with the medical evidence was returned'.

After conviction the rhetoric appeared and the *Liverpool Daily Post*[13] commented harshly:

> More uninteresting beings than the women sentenced on Saturday could not be imagined. Squalid, ignorant and showing by every glance and movement that brute-like sullenness which the life of

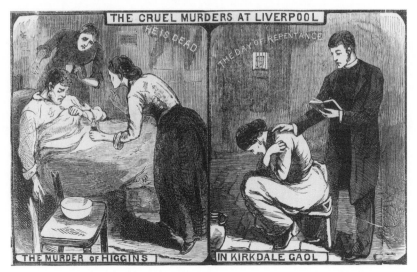

Illustrated Police News sketch showing the murder and the 'day of repentance' for Higgins.

courts and alleys stamps on the faces of those who live in it, these women went from house to house dealing death for a monetary gain not greater than that which the humblest avocation would have procured for them. How many their victims were and when they began their villainous trade probably will never be known.

The article covered many columns in similar vein, erroneously pursuing the theme that the financial gain was meagre.

The *Echo*[14] took a line more in tune with the theory propounded here, that 'these two women it may be with the aid of other persons have pursued a frightful career as slow poisoners'. The article went on to refer to them as 'The Lucretia Borgias of Modern Life' and 'Monsters in human shape' which is the type of rhetoric anticipated when the Victorian view of morality of women is recalled.

In conclusion it can be seen that there is a change in the way the press portrayed the sisters before and after conviction. Taking an overall view, those pre-trial reports are reasonably fair. There are vitriolic comments about both sisters, particularly Flanagan, after the trial, but not as much as might be expected, with a surprising lack of gender-specific criticism.

CHAPTER 6

⁂

Collusion and blind eyes

*'Social reformers were no match for the combined opposition of
the insurance companies and the working classes'*[1]

THERE WAS CLEARLY CLOSE INVOLVEMENT between neighbours,
not only in the caring aspect of women visiting the sick (as Mrs
Manville visited Thomas Higgins as he lay dying) but also the more
sinister aspects of events during some of those visits. Then there was a
financial side to relationships, with responsibility often being taken for
payment of another's life insurance premiums and subsequent ill-gotten
gains shared out when the insured died.

The murder trial was conducted on the basis that Flanagan and
Higgins were acting alone, yet this chapter will show they had previously
acted in concert with other women and there had been other victims. It
could be argued that in this respect there was a miscarriage of justice,
but although morally they should not have faced trial alone, overall, the
decision not to proceed against any other suspects was correct in all the
circumstances.

Quite apart from the other women who might or might not have been
insuring with a view to killing, it is worth looking at the culpability of
the insurance companies and the doctors. Also to be taken into account
is the availability of poisons and the establishment's failure to curtail
easy access to potentially lethal material.

Doctors

Either the doctors were negligent or they were completely deceived
by the clever acting and persuasion of the sisters and, like Dr Rafter,

'placed every confidence in Mrs Flanagan because she appeared to be very anxious' about her 'daughter' Maggie Jennings.[2] (She subsequently became her 'aunt' for the purposes of the death certificate.) Alternatively perhaps they felt they owed a lesser standard of care to the poor, or a sufficient difference in standard as to feel the need to state, as Dr Whitford did in his evidence at the committal proceedings,[3] that he treated Thomas Higgins in his capacity as district medical officer to the parish of Liverpool, a point he also made clear in his article on 8 March 1884 in *The Lancet*. Prosecuting counsel, Mr Aspinall, in his opening speech, also thought it of sufficient importance to mention 'Dr Whitford ... whose duty it was to attend to cases in the humbler class of life when he was sent for.'[4]

Either way, any embarrassment is masked by totally ignoring the lapses and turning them into positive self-congratulation. Dr Whitford excused his failure to spot Thomas Higgins' true ailment but capitalised on his involvement in the case by writing a learned article in *The Lancet*.[5]

An example of professional cronyism is illustrated in this extract from the *Liverpool Echo* on 15 December 1883.[6] When the sisters were brought before the stipendiary magistrate on 15 December for further evidence to be given in the committal proceedings relating to the murder of Thomas Higgins, the prosecuting solicitor, William Marks, addressed the court:

> Before continuing the evidence Mr Marks said he wished to correct a mistake which, after hearing evidence before the coroner yesterday, he found had occurred. He had stated in his opening on Thursday that the entire credit was due to Patrick Higgins, and that he went to the coroner, and that the coroner then him sent him to Dr Whitford. He (Mr Marks) had since found out from information received, and from the evidence of Patrick Higgins, that the real credit, though it was due to Higgins in the first instance, was really due to Dr Whitford, who was communicated with, first by Higgins, and who put Higgins in communication with the coroner; and consequently the credit really of bringing the matter to the knowledge of the proper officers of the law was due to the doctor. He was sorry that the doctor should not have had the credit given to him in the first instance, because he had rendered every assistance he could from the beginning to the police. He

made the post-mortem examination, and he was pretty nearly able to say what the poison was, although no analysis had then been made. The deceased was not one of Dr Whitford's private patients, but it was a parish case. He also wished to correct a misunderstanding which existed among a number of people. Dr Whitford certified for dysentery and he (Mr Marks) found from a variety of sources that an opinion prevailed that the doctor had certified for one thing, and that the man had died from another. That was not so, for where a man was suffering from poisoning from arsenic or any vegetable poisoning, such as bad fruit, that would bring on dysentery, so that poisoning from arsenic really was dysentery, and that the cause of death was correct as certified.

Mr Raffles, the stipendiary, then said to Mr Marks, 'It is only due to Dr Whitford that you should make that explanation, and I am very glad to hear it.'

To follow that argument to its logical conclusion, one might say that a doctor who failed to notice a large carving knife stuck between the shoulder blades of a deceased person was nevertheless correct in certifying death as being caused by a massive haemorrhage.

The editors of *The Lancet* were not so easily placated and one can detect muted criticism of Dr Whitford's diagnosis in one of the articles.[7] In reviewing the case generally the article states:

One symptom, diarrhoea, was so pronounced that the medical man who saw the case more than once certified to its being the cause of death: the proximate cause no doubt it was, but "dysentery" is a symptom common to so many diseases. We freely admit that under the circumstances Dr Whitford acted circumspectly. Nevertheless we cannot help regretting that, as the case appeared to him so problematical, he did not ask the friends for permission to make a post-mortem examination. Had he done so of course he would have been refused but the very refusal, and the manner in which it was made, would probably have aroused his suspicions and so have led to his demanding an inquest. It is always better to take into account the possibility of poisons entering into the causation of disease. Especially when the clinical phenomena are embarrassing and equivocal.

That criticism would not have had such a wide readership as the local newspapers so Dr Whitford's professional reputation locally would have remained intact. Even there, there is no suggestion that a better, prompter diagnosis might have saved Thomas' life.

In a very interesting comment made by Patrick Jennings to a reporter from the *Liverpool Echo*[8] he said Mrs Flanagan had told him that the medicine she and her sister were giving to Maggie was obtained from 'the Sixpenny Doctor's' in Walton Road. He continues that he 'thought at the time that her death was very strange and sudden and I went to the 'Sixpenny Doctor' and told him of my suspicions, but he ordered me out of the place and threatened to strike me with a stick'. These are not facts which would have been put forward in evidence so no issue is taken with the fact that it was not given on oath. Indeed, it has the ring of truth to it. Doctors were not then (nor indeed now) terribly keen on having their professional diagnoses challenged, especially not by an illiterate, unemployed Irishman. More amazing, therefore, in the light of that comment, is Patrick Higgins' tolerant reception by Dr Whitford after Thomas' death.

Although there was widespread criticism of the lax insurance rules there was no adverse public concern about the doctors' practice of signing death certificates without seeing the patient's body, and only muted criticism of their diagnostic skills, which in all four cases mentioned at the trial, were proved inaccurate.

In fairness to the medical profession of the time, however, it must be conceded that the doctors' reasonable preconceptions as to the lifestyles of the slum-dwellers would have played their part in misguiding them towards their erroneous diagnoses. They went to the poor households of the parish expecting to find undernourished patients in unsanitary conditions suffering from classic diseases of poverty such as pneumonia, bronchitis and dysentery. They expected to find subservient and co-operative relatives who would answer their simple questions truthfully and honestly to the best of their limited and ignorant ability. They did not expect the grief-stricken carer to be able to anticipate the doctor's questions so as to be able to describe convincingly the likely symptoms of a particular illness which they wanted the doctor to put on the death certificate when the inevitable occurred. Catherine Flanagan convinced Dr Rafter that Maggie Jennings was suffering from pneumonia by concentrating on Maggie's cough and producing suitable evidence, deliberately neglecting to tell him she was vomiting and purging.

We know now, by reading the accounts of the post-mortem examinations of John Flanagan junior, Maggie Jennings, Thomas Higgins and Mary Higgins, that all of them died from the effects of arsenic poisoning. Yet according to their doctors, they died, respectively, from bronchitis, pneumonia, dysentery and bronchitis, inflammation of lungs. Four deaths, wrongly diagnosed.

The most blatant example of misdiagnosis is shown on 22-year-old John Flanagan's death certificate. Dr Hill had diagnosed bronchitis but how he reached that conclusion must remain a mystery for at the post-mortem examination Dr Whitford found[9] 'no pleural adhesions or any indications of disease' and 'there were no indications of bronchitis'. Dr Lowndes agreed with Dr Whitford, noting from his own observations of the exhumed body that 'the heart and lungs' were 'healthy and well preserved'.[10]

Catherine Flanagan, in her statement to her solicitor, listed six more people whom she said had been poisoned. The police investigated each death thoroughly and indeed seemed to have been aware of the possibility of the murders before Flanagan's statement was made available to them. Taking her at her word and bearing in mind the contemporaneous police report's agreement (with the exception of Charles Mure) there seems to be little doubt that was so, yet what were the doctor's diagnoses? Dr Houlgrave certified that Emma Godfrey died of 'paralysis' and Dr Fisher decided Catherine Neillan died of 'morbis cordis' (heart failure). Dr Brown diagnosed Mure's death a result of 'coma consequent upon water on the brain' and later vacillated as to whether he could have been poisoned or not. Dr Hill thought Catherine O'Brien's death was as a result of 'paralysis and apoplexy'. Dr Fisher said Mary Donnelly's 'bronchitis' proved fatal and Mary Flanagan died of 'pneumonia', according to Dr Utting. They were all wrong.

So of the remaining list, gleaned from gossip and innuendo, did Catherine Flanagan's husband John really die of pneumonia on Midsummer's Day? How many others were there?

Availability of poisons for rats and other unwanted creatures
It had been well known for many years that arsenic and other poisons were readily available for nefarious purposes and this fact, combined

with the easy system of benefits operated by the burial clubs, had long been regarded as a scandal. A satirical sketch in *Punch* magazine, reproduced in *The Times*[11] in 1849, encapsulates the general awareness of the problem. This was roughly thirty-five years before these crimes were committed:

SCENE. *The shop of* Mr Upas, *chymist and druggist.* Bottles, *his assistant, behind the counter.*

Enter Widow Woman, *with infant in arms, seemingly in great distress.*

Widow (much agitated) 'Threepenn'orth of Laudanum, please Sir.'

Bottles 'Laudanum, Ma'am. Yes, Ma'am – Sixpenn'orth I think you said, Ma'am.'

Widow *(sighing)* 'Threepenn'orth. Threepence is all I have in the world!'

Bottles 'Sorry for it, Ma'am.'

(Serves her.) [Exit Widow *frantically.]*

Enter ragged Little Girl, *and several other persons of squalid, wretched and sinister appearance.*

Bottles 'Now then, little girl, what's for you?'

Girl 'Mother says, please will you let her have as much Arsenic as you can for twopence–halfpenny, to kill rats.'

Bottles 'Rats, eh? Father belong to a burial club?'

Girl 'Yes, Sir, please, Sir.'

Bottles 'So I thought.' *(Delivers the Arsenic.)*

[Exit Little Girl.]

Now Sir, what can I do for you? *(to a stranger with his face muffled and his hat over his eyes.)*

Stranger 'Thank'ee; I'll wait.'

Bottles (to several customers). 'You for Arsenic? – you? – you? – all of you Arsenic? Six Arsenics; and you; – oh! One Corrosive Sublimate.'

(Serves them out packets ready made up.)

[Exeunt with the poison.]

Stranger (*having watched them all out*). 'I want some of the
strongest poison you have got.'

Bottles 'Well, Sir, I think Prussic Acid will suit you better than
any.'

Stranger 'That smells, don't it?'

Bottles 'Why, yes, Sir. Probably Strychnine would answer your
purpose?'

Stranger 'Is that pretty stiffish?'

Bottles (*smiling*) 'Oh! yes, Sir. I should be sorry to take two
grains of it.'

Stranger 'Let's have half an ounce.'

Bottles 'Half an ounce, Sir? (*Weighs it out*) What is the next
article, Sir?'

Stranger 'Nothing.'

Bottles 'Allow me to tempt you with a little Belladonna; very
killing, Sir, I assure you. Or would you try our Digitalis?
I could recommend our Colchicum, Sir.'

Stranger 'No, no!'

Bottles 'Or anything in the Vitriol way, Sir?'

Stranger (*with an oath*) 'No, I tell you. The Strychnine will do
the job. Hand it over, will you, and make haste.'

Bottles 'Directly, Sir. (*Folds and presents the packet.*) Thank
you, Sir. (*Takes the money and sweeps it into the till. Exit
Stranger.*) Ha! A pretty good morning's work; and if
the undertakers don't get a job or two out of it – and
perhaps Jack Ketch too – I shall be astonished rayther.'

[*Exit.*]

In 1851 the Sale of Arsenic Act caused controversy when an extra clause,
restricting sales to adult males, was inserted. The implicit, insulting,
assumption that women were more disposed towards using poison than
men outraged the social philosopher John Stuart Mill,[12] and after much
lobbying the bill was passed which, among other things, restricted sales
to 'a person of full age'.[13] However, poison was traditionally the weapon
of the woman in the home: cheap to acquire and undetectable in the

days before chemical testing became reliable in the latter half of the nineteenth century. The 1851 Act went some way to curb the problem, but not far enough. In 1878 Ellen Heesom in Cheshire killed two of her children and her mother with arsenic after insuring them. William Lefley in Boston died after eating his wife's rice and arsenic pudding in 1884. She denied all knowledge of the additive but was nevertheless committed for trial for murder. *The Lancet* reported the case [14] in progress, surmising that the verdict would have to be murder by the wife or suicide by the victim. It is not known whether he was insured. Elizabeth Berry insured three of her relatives then poisoned them in 1887. Florence Maybrick was accused of using arsenic from flypapers in 1889 to kill her husband.

The discussions about reforms of the insurance laws, which occupied the minds of the Home Office draftsmen in the months following the Liverpool case,[15] are so detailed and long-winded that it is unlikely that the participants could have believed the problem was solely confined to Liverpool. Indeed it is noted that in the Report of the Friendly Societies' Registrar for 1876 (p. 22) he found that illegal over-insurance of children was practised in manufacturing districts to an 'enormous' extent. Further comments later in the document discuss the possibility of setting up a Parliamentary Commission to enquire into insurance illegalities but initially to confine its operations to the Liverpool area where, it was feared, the investigations might reveal a large amount of crime. This was exactly the type of 'fussy energy' envisaged by *The Lancet*[16] in an article about the sale of poisons.'It is amusing to note the occasional explosions of that fussy energy with which the authorities are animated in regard to the sale of poisons. When a conviction occurs instructions are issued to the police to enforce the law.' It goes on for some lines basically saying that the enthusiasm wanes after a few weeks and that the only effect the headlines have is to advertise the fact that poisons are so easily available, thus perpetuating the danger. This article does not specify any particularly bad area and therefore suggests a national problem. Whatever the results of those deliberations, Elizabeth Berry was able to insure and poison in 1887 (also in Liverpool as it happened) because, although certain loopholes had been closed, others remained.

Arsenic was commonly used in the manufacture of everyday products such as wallpaper and easily obtained by anyone working in paint manufacturing.[17] If sold in small quantities it had by law to be mixed with colouring of soot or indigo, 'ten pounds being the smallest quantity

A market pocket like that worn by Margaret Higgins, which contained traces of arsenic.

allowed to be sold unadulterated.'[18] Nevertheless, as the *Echo* pointed out, that safeguard was ineffective as it was 'a generally known fact' that flypapers contained arsenic and every summer thousands of flypapers were sold without query or check, and 'for 2*d*. or 3*d*.' anyone could obtain sufficient arsenic to kill. Liquid in a flask founn[19] in the cellar where Thomas Higgins died was analysed[20] and found to contain a solution of arsenic in water. Fluff in the market pocket[21] worn by Margaret Higgins[22] also contained traces of arsenic.[23] However, it may have been 'generally known' by the newspaper reporters and the working-class poor, but not, apparently, to Dr Campbell Brown.[24] He was the Liverpool City Analyst, Doctor of Science of University College, Liverpool; had lectured for fourteen years on toxicology at the Royal Infirmary School of Medicine, and had twenty years' experience of the detection of poisons. He gave evidence at the trial that he had been puzzled about the source of the arsenic used to kill the four victims. The day before he appeared in court he 'heard something' and made some experiments to test his new idea. He propounded his theory that arsenic had been obtained from flypapers. Of nine samples, eight contained arsenic and were easily soluble. From two of Liverpool manufacture he obtained a solution closely resembling the liquid found in the flask earlier produced in evidence. The reporter remarked that the prisoners, listening intently, 'never seemed in the least affected' by this revelation. With the wisdom of hindsight, it is obvious why not.

Mr Shee, counsel for the defence, in his closing speech[25] said it was 'hardly likely that these poor women would have learned to make a solution from flypaper and administer it in doses that would gradually kill.' Yet Catherine Flanagan's statement made before her conviction was nestling in his brief and so puts the lie to that submission and supports the *Daily Post*'s assertion that it was generally known. When Catherine Flanagan's solicitor, Mr Neale, wrote[26] to the Director of Public Prosecutions enclosing her statement, he emphasised his client's desire that 'for the benefit of the Public ... steps may be taken to prevent the wholesale circulation of Flypapers which are exceedingly dangerous to the community at large and from which the poison used by the convicts was obtained.'

It was a fact that arsenic was also used in medicine, but Mr George Greves, the dispenser at the Burlington Street parish dispensary, said on oath that it was 'at least eighteen months since I made up any arsenical medicine',[27] thereby refuting any suggestion that Thomas Higgins could have been poisoned by the medicine prescribed for him.

Insurance Companies

'To Hell with the clubs, you'll get no money for me!'[28]

To the Victorian poor, the dignity of a proper funeral was of paramount importance. To that end, burial societies provided the solution. A few pence each week, collected by the agent of the society would, in theory, guarantee avoidance of the dreaded pauper's burial. Agents would make weekly house calls, collecting premiums. Life insurance ranged from the respected large companies such as the Prudential Assurance Company, (who insured John Flanagan and Thomas Higgins), and the smaller but nevertheless honestly run British Workmen's Insurance Company (who insured Thomas and Mary Higgins and Maggie Jennings), to the unregistered friendly societies whose activities exploited the poorest in society by taking advantage of legal loopholes. These societies were, in the phraseology of a Home Office Memorandum[29] written in the spring of 1884, in the aftermath of the sisters' trial in Liverpool, 'Vast parasitical growths on the industry of the poor'. Even the more reputable societies were heavily criticised by the trial judge and the Home Office draftsmen whose memoranda and correspondence fill twenty close-typed pages, as they pondered the difficulties of trying to legislate against 'the laxity of the system' (p. 1 of that memo). As they well recognised, 'the main evil to be remedied is that of persons insuring the life of another in whose life they have no interest, for thus by taking out insurance they acquire an interest only in his death' (p. 2 of that memo). Mr Justice Butt, the trial judge, laid the blame for insurance malpractice on the paying of agents' commission on the premiums.

Small wonder then that collectors actively sought new members. An example of this practice is given in the witness statements of Mr Finegan, agent for the Prudential Assurance Company, at the inquest into the death of Thomas Higgins. It seems Flanagan was urged by her friend Mrs Stanton to 'find him a member or two it will help him'. Mrs Stanton paid some of the premiums on that particular policy on Thomas Higgins' life on Flanagan's behalf. Some collectors admitted in their evidence that it was customary to allow wives to sign for their husbands, to insure a life without that person knowing of the existence of the policy and even to make up details of the health and history of persons thus insured.

Criticism of insurance companies bordering on condemnation came from the press, medical journals and the lawyers involved in the trial.[30] Suggestions were made that it was their laxity in administration and procedures which allowed and even encouraged the unscrupulous to gain a pecuniary advantage by killing which, according to the *Manchester Examiner*,[31] was 'not an uncommon crime'. A very long article after conviction[32] suggested that killing for insurance benefit was an established custom: 'Many Flanagans employ the poison cup without fear of discovery'.

As early as 12 October 1883 the *Post* suggested insurance benefits were the motive for the untimely deaths of Thomas Higgins and Margaret Jennings.[33] Three days later[34] the accusation was repeated and accusations made of a series of insurance-motivated killings by Catherine Flanagan. The *Echo* commented[35] that insuring people without their knowledge was not uncommon 'in lower parts of this and other large towns' where 'family clubber' was a familiar phrase.

Mr John Bridge Aspinall, QC,[36] opening the case for the Crown, listed the various insurances taken out on Thomas' life and hinted at the 'great danger of these insurances'.[37]

His brother Clarke Aspinall was the Liverpool City Coroner who had dealt with all four inquests relating to the deaths of Thomas Higgins, Mary Higgins, Maggie Jennings and John Flanagan.

He had been appointed coroner on 29 August 1867 and, wishing to devote all his energy to that post, he resigned from partnership in his solicitor's firm, Aspinall & Bird. One of the problems which concerned him (and some of his fellow coroners) in his new post was the enormously high rate of infant deaths, particularly where those deaths were linked with burial clubs. A report in 1843[38] described the burial clubs as providing 'a bounty on neglect and infanticide'. In 1889[39] the Friendly Societies Select Committee Report concluded that 'allegations of culpable and even visible neglect or violence resulting in deaths of children were well founded'. Further research showed that things had not improved from the previous generation when nearly a quarter of the known deaths by poisoning had been children under the age of five.[40]

In 1892 Dr F. W. Lowndes,[41] who had performed the post-mortem examination on Maggie Jennings, John Flanagan junior and Mary Higgins, argued that the office of coroner should be held by a doctor, rather than a lawyer because[42] 'there were many cases of poisoning where the verdict was that the deceased had died from "a visitation of God" simply because the coroner, not being a medical man did not recognise the symptoms'.

It was common knowledge that children were insured several times over in different burial clubs and friendly societies. Clarke Aspinall considered that the existence of burial societies or clubs did have an unfavourable effect on the mortality rates of infants and urged that proven neglect should entitle the society or club to refuse payment.'Children and adults are often in several clubs not infrequently in no way interested in anything but the money result of the death.'[43]

Throughout all the court proceedings, agents for various insurance companies gave lengthy evidence as to how the policies came to be taken out, the amounts, claims and demeanours of the prisoners. Overall,[44] it is clear the agents were so anxious for business that they flouted standard practices for checking and approving those whose lives were to be insured.

The stipendiary magistrate for Liverpool, Mr Raffles, commented 'What a farce this seeing and passing must be' on hearing evidence from one of the insurance representatives who, on seeing Thomas Higgins' body, realised it was not the same man to whom he had been presented when Thomas' life insurance proposal was accepted.[45]

It was clear even at the committal and inquest stage of the proceedings that some agents were acting at the least improperly, and in some cases forging and falsifying documents. Richard Jones,[46] an agent for the Royal Liver Friendly Society, filled in a proposal form according to answers given to him by Margaret Higgins. The policy was never validated because Thomas Higgins, when Mr Jones eventually tracked him down, refused to co-operate. The form is headed 'Questions to be answered by the person on whose life the assurance is proposed'. One of the questions was 'Have your parents brothers or sisters been healthy and long lived or otherwise?' and the answer given was 'Have no relation living'. Yet he had his brother Patrick living ten minutes' walk away. (The question 'Are there any brothers or sisters living?' gets a 'Yes' on a different proposal form, completed by agent Samuel Finegan.)[47]

John Bowles of the Pearl Assurance Company[48] admitted at the trial that a month elapsed before he realised that Ellen Flanagan, supposedly signing on behalf of Margaret Higgins, had actually signed 'Thomas Higgins'. He said when cross-examined at the trial that he made it his practice to look at signatures to proposals (he failed to do so on this occasion) and continued 'when the proposal was signed I had no suspicion'. He parried a few searching questions from the judge who eventually squeezed from him the admission that 'so far as I know, the man (Thomas Higgins) did not know his life was being insured'. He was followed into the witness box by Frances Bowles[49] who said that on 2 October 1883 he saw the policy the last witness had produced but 'could not say where it had been before that time', eliciting the comment from the judge: 'There are a great many strange things about these policies.'

Mr Bennett, collector for the Wesleyan and General, said[50] he took the proposal on Thomas Higgins' life and that the cross to the name 'Thomas Higgins' was put on 'by a man whom the prisoner[51] told me was Higgins.' (It is not clear which sister he meant by 'prisoner'.) In answer to a series of questions by the judge, Bennett said he knew of no cases where insurance was effected by a wife without her husband knowing. He was not asked about his suspicions.

Comment in the *Liverpool Echo*[52] during the trial made the point that the system of insurance was lax. It cited as an example a collector who deliberately avoided speaking to Thomas Higgins fearing his disapproval, used his imagination to complete the form about his medical and personal history, and then forged Thomas Higgins' signature.[53] This evidence was given amidst laughter. The judge asked him if he realised he was committing forgery and he ingenuously responded, 'I never filled up forms for our office in any way but that'. Another agent, asked if he thought it right for a wife to sign her husband's name, said he'd have no objection if his wife signed for him. This caused much amusement in the courtroom. The judge[54] blamed this type of malpractice on paying agents commission on the premiums: 'That is at the bottom of it all'. Mr George Griffith, agent for the Scottish Legal Life Assurance Company, had told the court that he received the first eight weeks' premiums and twenty-five per cent commission from then onwards.[55]

When prosecuting counsel, Mr Aspinall,[56] rose to make his closing speech to the jury he referred to the conduct of many of the agents of the insurance societies as 'perfectly shocking', saying they afforded 'dangerous opportunities' to the prisoners, putting them in a position of 'strong temptation'.

His opponent, Mr Shee, played down the insurance motive[57] saying that the point 'was a small one as it was a common thing to insure relatives and what was more, the canvassers were persistent in pressing people to insure their friends.'

The judge[58] in summing up harshly condemned the insurance system as 'vicious' and responsible for no end of iniquities.

The Echo[59] hoped that Mr Justice Butt's strong remarks about the way insurances were effected would have repercussions 'in the proper quarter' and commented that the subject was certainly one that called for serious reform. It urged the Secretary of State to see that temptations were not put in the way of people like the two prisoners by abuse of the management of insurance societies and burial clubs. Their intentions were good but the paper urged reforms in their manner of business.

After the verdict the Liverpool Daily Post[60] on 18 February 1884 reported severe criticism of insurance societies and burial clubs from the defence, prosecution and the judge, emphasising the inherent dangers:

> ... among the squalid poor the blankness of life destroys the conception of its sacredness. Those whose lives are worth living seldom have much compunction in destroying the lives of others. A tradition of successful crime operates powerfully among the wretched and ignorant. In the dense quarters of a great town, to

kill secretly is far from difficult and the advantages which may be reaped from murder are very obvious. It is to be feared that these women pursued an avocation by no means uncommon and one which has created traditions which they for years supplied with impunity. Society does not investigate too curiously into the deaths of its worthless members. A few pence will procure poison enough to destroy many lives, and very slight care in its employment will diminish the probabilities of detection. The story is told of a bystander watching the coffins of three children borne down the street to burial. A ragged woman looking on, exclaims with a sigh 'Ah me, some people have luck'. Whether true or not, the anecdote reveals a true state of affairs. To hundreds of thousands of persons in this country the death of a child means 'luck' and, what is worse, the poison soaked from a few flypapers will bring 'luck' to those who seek for it. So long as it is profitable to poison, and there are those degraded enough to reap such profit, no precautions will prevent the commission of crimes such as that of the woman Flanagan, or will secure the detection when once committed.

It then continues with direct accusations at the burial societies: 'The luck for which the ragged woman of the story sighed came from the burial club and friendly society. In the trial of last week, these institutions, admirable enough in themselves, kept modestly and judiciously in the background.' The article reminded its readers of instances where the burial clubs or insurance societies had refused to pay, not being satisfied as to the circumstances of the relevant death, and yet made no further enquiries. The conclusion was that 'The women, grumbling, went away and the loss was made up by the murder of a new victim.' Demands were made for the tightening of rules to prevent the unscrupulous killing for insurance profit and the article concluded: 'The temptation to make away with young children is great and is one which probably is more frequently yielded to than most people care to believe ... if the practice of poisoning is to be rooted out from among the ignorant classes, the methods of these burial and friendly societies must undergo a radical reform.'

This reinforces the argument that the practice of insuring and poisoning was rife. *The Lancet* entered into the debate[61] and opined that insurance practices were 'open temptations to murder' and continued, 'we trust that recent experience may serve as a warning to the Legislature and an admonition to the Executive'. In another article[62] it suggested that 'no life assurance office ought to insure a life without examining the subject'. Perhaps it might also have looked introspectively at the medical profession and suggested that no doctor ought to certify a death without seeing the body, but it did not, and recent events confirm that the practice still continues.[63] It was, as *The Lancet* said, common practice to dispense with this and difficult to enforce a law making it mandatory. It suggested that an act be passed making the person whose life was to be insured countersign a policy in the presence of witnesses, thereby preventing very young children being insured and by so doing 'putting an end to a very disastrous facility for fraud and murder'.

In the aftermath of the trial when the Home Office, DPP and Treasury Solicitor were investigating the other deaths, all of which were linked with insurances, the Treasury Solicitor wrote to the Home Office, 'It is certain that of the agents of the insurance companies – who are not disposed to assist the police in any way – enquiry cannot safely be made.'[64] The insurance companies were clearly on the defensive, and the Royal Liver Friendly Society, anxious to avoid bad publicity, went to the lengths of instructing two counsel to represent them at the inquest into Thomas' death,[65] merely to convince the court (and more importantly the press) that the deceased had not been insured by those instructing them. Theirs was the policy which had not been ratified because, as we have already seen, Thomas took such exception to the further insuring of his life that he angrily dismissed Mr Jones, the agent from the Royal Liver.[66]

There was a clear intention on the part of the Home Office to tighten the regulations. The Treasury Solicitor was instructed to report on the situation and in a letter he writes,[67] 'In accordance with the desire of the Secretary of State expressed to me verbally I will shortly report specifically as to the practices of the insurance companies in Liverpool which have come to light in this case.'[68]

In essence, the companies and agents bore a share of liability for the deaths of the victims. They, like Flanagan and Higgins, acted in pursuit of money. Had their procedures been tighter, their integrity greater and their agents less reliant on commission for their earnings, prospects for the unscrupulous would have been bleak.

Why insure the life of a young healthy person who is no financial liability? There can be only one reason, a chilling one.

꧁ ꧂

CHAPTER 7

The Poisoning Syndicate

'These two women, it may be with the aid of other persons, have
for some years pursued a frightful career as slow poisoners.'

Liverpool Echo, 18 February 1884

O N 18 February 1884 when the trial had concluded, the *Liverpool Echo* asserted that 'others' were going to be arrested in connection with the murders. No doubt that was expected but events did not prove the reporter correct.

On 22 February 1884 Catherine Flanagan's solicitor, Mr Neale, sent a copy of a statement made by to her while she was in Kirkdale Gaol before conviction. In it she names a number of accomplices, some of whom were surely worthy of further investigation.

Statement of Catherine Flanagan and covering letter from her
solicitor (Documents in file PRO, HO 144/126 A33023/10)
The Queen *v.* Catherine Flanagan and Margaret Higgins
For Murder
   Statement of Prisoner Catherine Flanagan
   H. F. Neale, Solicitor, Liverpool.

25 Dale Street, Liverpool
22 February 1884

   Sir J. B. Maule Q.C., Director of Public Prosecutions,
   Whitehall, London, S.W.
Sir,
Reg. *v.* Flanagan and Higgins
The above named persons now lie at Kirkdale Gaol Liverpool

under sentence of death for the wilful murder of Thomas Higgins by arsenic poisoning.

I acted for the prisoner Flanagan as her Solicitor upon her Trial and *before her conviction* [my emphasis] she made to me a statement a copy of which I have the honour to enclose.

The convict has given me full power to deal with it in such manner as I may think advisable consistently with her desire that for the benefit of the Public such other persons may be brought to justice as it may tend to convict in case if sufficient evidence can be obtained to justify such conviction and also in order that steps may be taken to prevent the wholesale circulation of Flypapers which are exceedingly dangerous to the community at large and from which the poison used by the convicts was obtained.

I have handed a copy of the statement referred to to Mr W. Marks, Prosecuting Solicitor, Liverpool, but I have also thought it my duty to communicate the same to you.

I have the honour to be Sir,

Your Obedient Servant,

H. F. Neale

Catherine Flanagan says:

I admit that I had knowledge of poison being administered to the persons whose death I am now charged with causing, but I deny that I administered it myself in either one case or the other. The person who is responsible for the inception of the crime is Margaret Evans a Fish-woman living in Blenheim Street. Mrs Hoare knows her. A woman named Catherine Neillan formerly lived with her in Kew Street and was assured by her (Evans) and two other women named Margaret Potter and Mrs Fallon. (Hoare knows them all) My sister Margaret Higgins then lived with Evans and she has since told me that she and Evans poisoned the girl Neillan and that Evans obtained the poison. Evans and my sister Higgins both attended on her and they used Flypaper water. A woman named Catherine O'Brien the wife of Hugh O'Brien, a labourer lived in a Court in Blenheim Street. Evans had her insured. Catherine Ryan keeps a Coal Yard in St Martin Street and one occasion I was in the Druggists Shop at the

corner of Burlington Street when she got some poison. I do not
know what it was but it was of a light blue colour. She gave me
the packet to give to Evans and I did so. Evans said to me 'I want
money and I must have it and I am going out to see a young
fellow who is sick.' She also told me his name was 'Mule' or
something like that and that he lived beyond Bootle, at Seaforth
I believe. He died soon after her visit but I cannot say what
she got by his death. I know that she has his father in clubs.
I saw Evans make up some of the powder I have mentioned
and give it to Catherine O'Brien who died on the following day.
I was present when she mixed and administered it and I said
to her 'What are you doing?' She said, 'Shut your mouth.' Mrs
Stanton and I both had O'Brien insured. Stanton got £29 by
the death but I forget what I received. My sister Higgins first
used Flypaper water to Mary Donnelly who was my son's wife's
mother and who died in St Martin Street about 4 or 5 years ago.
She was insured by a good few. Her daughter (my Son's wife,
Mary Flanagan) had her insured and gave Higgins £10 out of
the money after her death. I think the second person was my
son John's wife Mary Flanagan who was insured by my son. He
drew £20 from the Prudential Society. She died in Epsom Street.
Higgins gave her a dose and got £4 off my son after her death.
My son John followed and he was insured by me but Higgins
poisoned him and got a share of the money. Mary Higgins was
not insured by me at all and I positively assert that I had no
knowledge whatever that poison had been given to her until my
sister told me of it after her death. She was very ill and I thought
she died naturally. Higgins administered the poison which killed
Margaret Jennings. She always obtained the papers and mixed
and administered the poison and got me to make the assurances
and attend on the people until they died. I never at any time gave
poison to Thomas Higgins although I knew well what was going
on. The liquid I threw behind the fire was Brandy and there was
not more than a teaspoonful in the cup. All the insurances on
his life made by me were made at the request of his wife whom
I represented at her request. I do not think Mrs Stanton knew
anything about the poisoning although she may have suspected
something wrong. She never saw poison to my knowledge and

never that I am aware of had anything to do with the administration of it. The only other death produced by poison which
I can remember now was that of 'Ellen' or 'Elizabeth' Godfrey
who died at Owen Begley's in St Martin Street about three years
ago. She was insured by Mrs Begley and by me and Mrs Begley
drew the claims but I do not know how much she got. Mrs
Begley knew what was used to kill and I have seen her mix and
administer the poison to Godfrey who died soon afterwards. I
again repeat that I never personally administered poison to any
of the deceased persons. My sister instigated the murders and
attended upon the victims in each instance except Godfrey and
O'Brien. She always administered the poison and I only attended
in her absence in order that suspicion might not be aroused by
the symptoms produced.

In his letter dated 25 February 1884[1] the prosecuting solicitor for
Liverpool, William Marks, told the DPP that he felt that the six people
referred to in Catherine Flanagan's statement were probably poisoned,
but he acknowledged that it would be very difficult to prove anyone other
than Flanagan and Higgins responsible.

He revealed that before the trial Flanagan, through her solicitor Mr
Neale,[2] had expressed her willingness to testify against her sister, clearly
with a view to obtaining clemency. Her offer was refused. He continued
that he was of the opinion that Flanagan and Higgins were the
ringleaders in the series of murders. The main difficulty was that both
sisters had access to five of the six victims, the exception being Charles
Mure. He thought it likely that Ellen Flanagan, Catherine's 14-year-old
daughter, could give 'valuable information' and had reason to believe
she would be willing so to do but only after her mother's execution.
Unfortunately no further information can be gleaned about either
why he believed that or what happened subsequently. He concludes
his letter: 'I think it would have a bad effect if a prosecution were
instigated against any fresh prisoners and they were acquitted.' In
that sentence he encapsulates the prosecution's view; they had two
prisoners convicted, they were probably the ringleaders and there the
matter would end. Perhaps the sisters were scapegoats, but guilty ones,
nevertheless. Evidence against the other women was scant and relied
heavily on such testimony as Catherine Flanagan was prepared to give.

As the DPP and the Home Secretary were aware, she would only testify if promised clemency; she was involved with most of the murders herself and the cogency of her evidence would thereby diminish. The end result would probably have been an acquittal for the other suspects and life imprisonment for Catherine Flanagan, with Margaret Higgins still liable for capital punishment, an unsatisfactory conclusion, whichever way one regarded it. Weighing everything objectively, the decision not to pursue other possible syndicate members can be seen as the right one.

It is appropriate, however, to consider here who else was involved and what degree of blame they carry. There was a widespread network of insurance fraud and poisoning which seems to have been part of the mores of the class and period. There is a suggestion, in a letter from the Treasury Solicitor to the Home Office,[3] that there were even more women involved than Catherine Flanagan initially named in her statement.'Flanagan has since given a number of names to a female warder as of women concerned in poisoning but no particulars.' This tends to reinforce the theory that the practice was more widespread than has previously been acknowledged. After conviction the *Echo*[4] reported that 'these two women, it may be with the aid of other persons, have for some years pursued a frightful career as slow poisoners.'

Most of the people involved as witnesses and suspects lived within a small area in the north of Liverpool roughly bounded by Great Homer Street to the east, Vauxhall Road to the west, Boundary Street to the north and Burlington Street to the south. By noting the addresses of witnesses and suspects given at the time of the trial with the census returns for 1871 and 1881 it is clear that there was much movement of families within that tight community. Lodgers, some of whom were to become victims, moved between the families whose lives are central to this account.

Although this research is confined to Liverpool, the general remarks quoted above from the Home Office, DPP, Treasury Solicitor and press reports of the era do not suggest that it was a local phenomenon. It is unlikely that such swingeing reforms of the insurance laws and poison sales would have been embarked upon had that been the case.

A TANGLED WEB

It seems clear that there were many more people than the two sisters involved in the insurance and killing of both the proven and possible victims. The evidence, both documentary and circumstantial, is at best patchy, often inconclusive and always mind-boggling. What follows is my attempt to sift through it all to try to assess who might have been culpable and to what degree. I apologise in advance for the complexity of the material, which occasionally made even my head spin!

There are two women in particular whose names appear in the documents with alarming regularity: Margaret Evans and Bridget Stanton.

Margaret Evans

It is Margaret Evans whom Catherine Flanagan blames for beginning the series of poisonings.[5] She describes her as a fishwoman living in Blenheim Street but she has proved difficult to locate on the census and thus her age, marital condition and nationality remain uncertain.[6] There is a possible trace of her in the 1871 census living at 4 House, 12 Court, 22 St Martin Street, aged 40, widow, occupation hawker, born in Ireland. The only other person living with her was Elizabeth Evans, aged 6 years, born in Lancashire. There is a possible census trace of her in 1881 at 93 Prince Edwin Street, aged 54, born Liverpool, a shopkeeper, married. Next door is a fishmonger, which could link with Flanagan's description of her as a fishwife. Either or neither could be the right woman.

She is certainly an associate of the two sisters and the solicitor to the Treasury warned the Home Office in his letter[7] that Evans and her cohorts would abscond at the least hint of police activity, and cautioned that the police must move 'very circumspectly'. Probably he was naïve in believing they were not already aware of his recent visit to Liverpool and the enquiries that he and the police officers were making. She was accused by Flanagan in her statement[8] of complicity in four murders, the first being that of Charles Emmanuel Mure (the only case which does not involve Flanagan or Higgins). Catherine describes how Catherine Ryan purchased poison and gave it to her with instructions to pass it to Margaret Evans. Evans then told Flanagan, 'I want money and I must have it and I am going to see a young fellow who is sick.' The 'young fellow' was allegedly Charles Mure and that night he was taken violently ill with diarrhoea and vomiting. After that Evans visited almost daily, often with Mrs Stanton. Flanagan told her solicitor that Margaret Evans had insured both young Charles and his father but she did not know how much Evans claimed on the policy after his death.[9]

Curiously, a woman called Elizabeth Muir was buried in a public grave at Ford Cemetery on 8 March 1881 aged 44, having resided at her death at 19 Blenheim Street. In the 1881 census a Catherine Evans aged 52, born Ireland, lived at that address with her husband Martin, a chemical labourer and two other families. There is probably no connection whatsoever, merely a coincidence.

Interestingly, the Treasury Solicitor[10] did not believe the boy was poisoned at all and favoured the theory that 'the weakly are selected for insurance'. He thought Flanagan misinterpreted the comment Evans made about 'getting money quickly' (having just acquired poison) and seemed more inclined to the father's belief in that respect. Yet the mother's evidence, set out in the chapter relating to the victims, is surely indicative of malpractice. From the evidence available[11] it is clear that Evans had motive, means and opportunity.

Margaret Evans, along with Mrs Potter and Mrs Fallon, insured the life of Catherine Neillan who lived with her and Margaret Higgins (then Thompson) in Kew Street. Catherine Flanagan alleged that her sister told her she and Evans poisoned Neillan, using 'flypaper water'.[12] Inspector Boyes' report[13] confirms that Neillan was lodging with Margaret Higgins and Evans at 39 Kew Street when she died. Maria Hoare the undertaker went further,[14] saying that Neillan had not lodged there more than three months prior to her death.

On the death of Margaret Jennings[15] it was probably Margaret Evans who accompanied Mrs Flanagan when she attended the offices of the Crown and Anchor Burial Society to claim on Maggie's life assurance policy. It was certainly Evans who applied for the death certificate, appending her cross over her name on the application form.[16]

Catherine O'Brien was living in Blenheim Street when she died and was visited by Evans, Flanagan and Mary Carroll.[17] Catherine Flanagan alleges that O'Brien was insured by her, Mrs Stanton and Evans.[18] More damagingly, she says, 'I saw Evans make up some powder and give it to O'Brien,' who died the next day. When she asked her what she was doing, Evans told her to 'shut your mouth'. Perhaps Flanagan misinterpreted that as well?

Insurance features in all cases, and in each case one or other of the women are involved: Mrs Carroll, Mrs Fallon, Mrs Stanton, Margaret Higgins or Catherine Flanagan herself. Evans was also one of the witnesses for Flanagan in her slander action[19] against Maria Hoare, demonstrating again the support which Catherine Flanagan was able to call upon and exemplifying the type of comradeship which Ellen Ross describes in her work on community networks.[20]

My conclusion is that Margaret Evans was deeply involved and should have been brought to trial alongside the sisters.[21]

Bridget Stanton

Mrs Bridget Stanton was the wife of Thomas. The surname is sometimes referred to as Staunton but for convenience I will refer to her as Stanton. It has proved difficult to establish her identity and although there are many references to her, she cannot be definitively pinpointed on either the 1871 or the 1881 census.[22] There is a Bridget Staunton listed in the 1881 census as living three doors away from Flanagan and Higgins at 136 Blenheim Street. Whether or not this is the correct woman is debatable. She is listed as wife of Thomas, aged 30, labourer, she being 23 years old. Both were born in Liverpool as were their three children, aged 10, 8 and 6. Their mother's age is clearly wrong, as often happened on the census returns. There are no other couples, Thomas and Bridget, listed in that census either as Staunton or Stanton. However, in the 1871 census for Liverpool, Thomas Stanton, labourer, aged 27 and Bridget aged 23 are living in Blenheim Street, 47, Court 19, both born in Ireland.

She is known to have been a close companion of Margaret Evans[23] and the Treasury Solicitor cautions against seeing her lest Evans learns of the enquiries.

Catherine specifically excludes Mrs Stanton from involvement in precise yet curious terms:[24] 'I do not think Mrs Stanton knew anything about the poisoning although she may have suspected something wrong. She never saw poison to my knowledge and never that I am aware of had anything to do with the administration of it.' Yet Mrs Stanton appears everywhere, particularly where insurances are concerned, sometimes paying the premiums herself on behalf of Catherine Flanagan. So far as Thomas Higgins[25] was concerned she urged Catherine Flanagan to insure him, paying those premiums herself[26] (or some of them),[27] and allowing Mrs Flanagan to be paid the subsequent claim in her house, 54

Buckingham Street, on 4 October 1883.[28] Mrs Stanton's name appears on the claim form, certifying the identity of Thomas, recently deceased, giving her Christian name as 'Margaret' and appending her signature. (It appears from another insurance document[29] that Bridget Stanton was illiterate, marking her cross by her name.) Flanagan, pretending to be Margaret Higgins, made her mark alongside the name 'Margaret Higgins' and both signatures were witnessed by Mr Finegan, the Prudential agent.[30]

Catherine Flanagan[31] alleged that Stanton had insured Catherine O'Brien and received £29 on her death. Maria Hoare[32] also said that Mrs Stanton had insured Catherine O'Brien.

Mrs Stanton was also a proposer for the life of Maggie Jennings.[33] She made a verbal proposal (which was acceptable for amounts under £25) on 28 October 1882 in the sum of £24 12s. 0d. with the Crown and Anchor Assurance and Burial Society. The policy was for the benefit of an unnamed aunt. Mrs Stanton also paid those premiums on behalf of 'the aunt'.[34] As it happened, Maggie died after only thirteen weeks' premiums had been paid and therefore no payment was due on her death. Mrs Flanagan and another woman went to claim on the policy and were refused payment, but because of her plea of poverty Mrs Flanagan was given a grant of 10s.[35]

Inspector Boyes,[36] investigating the allegations made by Catherine Flanagan in her statement, failed to trace a sale of poison to Catherine Ryan but found instead a record in the chemist's shop at the corner of Burlington Street referring to Thomas Stanton, Bridget's husband. He had purchased rat poison, in a blue powder form, on 15 September 1882. Bridget Stanton accompanied Mrs Evans on three visits to see Charles Mure.[37]

Mrs Stanton was clearly under suspicion by the police and was arrested but released without charge.[38] Incidentally, Thomas Stanton was a witness at the marriage of Thomas Higgins and Margaret, then Thompson. The other witness was Ellen Flanagan.[39]

Even Ellen Flanagan distances Mrs Stanton from the poisoning and insurance,[40] saying 'I do not remember Mrs Stanton taking any policies away. She had not that much acquaintance with my mother.' (She was 'aquainted' with Catherine Flanagan well enough to allow her home to be used to host the pay-out on Thomas Higgins' life insurance, acquiescing in Flanagan's pretence that she was the new Widow Higgins.)[41] Yet, even accepting the inherent unreliability of the press, contrast Ellen's denial with this report:[42]

> Mrs Stanton, who was referred to by us in yesterday's *Daily Post* as having seized all the insurance policies and other documents belonging to Mrs Flanagan shortly after that woman's flight, appears to be a moneylender in a small way, a class to which her friend, the absconding person, belonged and which we find is numerously represented among the labouring classes in the city.

If Ellen was asked whether Mrs Stanton took policies away, it is reasonable to suppose the questioner was hoping for an affirmative answer, which leads to the conclusion that it was suspected she had.

Samuel Finegan, insurance agent for the Prudential Assurance Company[43] was introduced to Catherine Flanagan by Bridget Stanton when he met the two women in the street one day. Mrs Stanton explained he was 'her clubman' and, it will be remembered, urged Flanagan to 'find him a member or two, it will help him'. It was at her persuasion that Catherine Flanagan insured her 'husband' Thomas Higgins. Mrs Stanton obligingly paid some of the premiums.[44] Until the revelations after Thomas' death, Mr Finegan was, apparently, under the impression that Catherine Flanagan was Margaret Higgins, and clearly Mrs Stanton did not disabuse him of this error. On one occasion when he went looking for 'Mrs Higgins' he asked Bridget Stanton where she had gone to.[45]

Mrs Stanton then came out with some bad language, saying she and Mrs Higgins had fallen out. One assumes that she meant the real Mrs Higgins, whereas poor Mr Finegan was looking for the elder sister. Certainly, Flanagan and Stanton were friendly enough after Thomas' death. Finegan went to Stanton's house, which he says was 34 Buckingham Street, to pay out to Catherine £7 11s. 6d. on 4 October 1883. He was still under the impression that she was the new widow Higgins; Stanton again (one assumes she was in a position to hear the conversation in her own house) did not contradict when the 'widow' was talking of her late husband's sudden death.[46]

There is a reference to Mrs Stanton in a Home Office Memorandum relating to problems of the insurance business and their possible remedies.[47] It alleges that when Flanagan and Higgins went to claim benefit due from the Scottish Legal Life Assurance Company, Margaret

Higgins called herself Mrs Stanton and Catherine Flanagan called herself Margaret Higgins. At first sight it is difficult to see how the writer came to this conclusion, and in fairness to Mrs Stanton what happened in her absence cannot be held against her. However, looking at the evidence at the committal of William Cartwright,[48] District Manager, he says he paid the benefit on Thomas' life to Catherine Flanagan, she telling him after some persuasion by the other woman present that her name was Margaret Higgins. Flanagan played the grieving widow saying she 'had lost the best husband in the world', then put her cross to the name Margaret Higgins on the receipt.[49] The other name on the form is Bridget Stanton, marked with a cross.

In his evidence before the coroner,[50] however, he goes further and states: 'I never saw the woman Higgins till I saw her in the court,' making it quite clear that the other woman with Flanagan was not Margaret Higgins. However, at the trial, it is not Cartwright but William Parker who gave evidence on behalf of the Scottish Legal Life Assurance Company, he describing himself as Manager. He said he made the payment, there being three women present, 'the two prisoners and another woman'. He, like Cartwright, repeats the scene where Flanagan pretends to be Higgins, but names Mrs Stanton as the one who persuades her to do so.[51]

If indeed it was Mrs Stanton who took part in the charade it surely indicates complicity in, at least, the insurance fraud. Going further, her involvement with insurance on those people who died very suddenly, with the same symptoms – Thomas Higgins, Maggie Jennings, Charles Mure and Catherine O'Brien – must indicate at best an unbelievable naïvety and at worst full involvement.

Mrs Stanton was clearly under suspicion by the police and was arrested but released without charge.[52]

The conclusion is that she too was heavily involved but the evidence is weaker than against Evans,[53] mainly because, for some strange reason, Catherine Flanagan exonerates her.

Margaret Potter, Mrs Fallon and Bridget Pugh

Little is known about Margaret Potter or Mrs Fallon apart from the allegation by Catherine Flanagan in her statement[54] that they insured Catherine Neillan who died on 4 April 1880 while living with Margaret Evans and Margaret Higgins. Mrs Potter may be she 'of Tenterden Street' referred to by Maria Hoare in her statement to the *Echo*;[55] if so she was a friend of Catherine Flanagan and stood as a witness for Flanagan in the slander action.

Mrs Hoare, in her statement to the police,[56] confirms that Mrs Fallon had told her 'that she had had Neillan in a club, but not long'. Similarly, little is known about Bridget Pugh other than a fragment courtesy of Maria Hoare,[57] that she lived in Blenheim Street and had insured Catherine O'Brien. There is no evidence to link these three women with anything other than financial gain on life insurances.

Bridget Begley

There is a considerable amount of evidence that Bridget Begley was actively involved in malpractice. There are clear interactions between Flanagan, Begley, Ryan and Evans. According to Maria Hoare,[58] Mrs Begley's husband Owen stood as a witness for Catherine Flanagan in her slander action. At the time of the 1871[59] census Bridgett and her husband Owen lived at No 4 house, 12 Court, 22 St Martin Street, Liverpool, with Margaret Evans. In the 1881 census[60] they are listed at 34 St Martin Street next door to Catherine Ryan. Bridget is listed as aged 42 with husband Owen aged 40, a dock labourer. Both were born in Ireland with three sons all born in Liverpool.

In Catherine's statement[61] she says she saw Begley mixing and administering poison to Emma Godfrey who died soon after. She says she and Begley both had her insured. Maria Hoare stated that Godfrey was living with the Begleys at 33 St Martin Street[62] when she died, and she told the police[63] that she undertook the funeral at the requests of Flanagan and Mrs Begley, both of whom had Godfrey insured. She adds: 'I heard she was poisoned.' Inspector Boyes confirms in his report[64] that Godfrey did indeed live with the Begleys at her death but gives a different address, 27 St Martin Street. He quotes evidence of Mrs McNamara then living in the cellar of that house who saw Mrs Flanagan (not Mrs Begley, although she was present) give poison to Godfrey. Inspector Boyes says the death certificate shows Mrs Begley as 'cousin' of the deceased and that she was present at the death, neither fact being true. The view of the Treasury Solicitor[65] as set out in his letter of 1 March 1884 to the Home Office minister is that he believed Godfrey was poisoned but found himself unable to take further steps because of Flanagan's involvement and lack of corroboration of her evidence.

He came to the conclusion that it was an isolated case for Begley and all they could prove was her presence in her own home. This was the only sensible decision, but taking an overview she was clearly involved in the macabre practice. There is no direct evidence of actual poisoning by one or other woman, but there is evidence of false declaration by Begley[66] on the death certificate and joint enterprise with Flanagan over the insurance[67] aspect of Godfrey's death.

Mary Carroll

Mary Carroll is another shadowy figure. Looking at the 1881 census,[68] there is a Mary Carroll aged 38 living at 28 Telary Street which is near Latimer Street, and if it is this woman then she is listed as being born in Ireland, as were her husband, two children and one lodger. Her husband Richard aged 39 worked as a 'chemical labourer'. According to Inspector Boyes' report[69] she was the sister-in-law of Catherine Flanagan. She, Flanagan and Mrs Evans visited Catherine O'Brien during her illness before her death in April 1882. In his letter[70] to the Home Office, the Treasury Solicitor Mr Cuffe reported that Mary Carroll was one of those 'suspected of malpractice' and for some reason that is not clear she features high on his list of suspects. It could possibly be because of her associate, Evans, and her relationship to Flanagan. It could also be because of her husband's occupation, but that is mere speculation on my part. However, there was no evidence against her and Flanagan does not accuse her in her statement.

Catherine Ryan

So far as Catherine Ryan is concerned there is no solid evidence but a plethora of coincidences give rise to suspicion. Catherine Flanagan, in her statement,[71] identifies her as keeping a coal yard in St Martin Street. The 1871 census lists her at 28 St Martin Street, aged 32, with her husband, Martin, aged 30, a shipping dock labourer. Both were born in Ireland. By 1881[72] they had moved to 32 St Martin Street next to Bridget Begley who lived at 34. Her age is given as 35, which does not correlate to the previous census return, but her husband has correctly aged ten years. They are listed with five children and three lodgers.

Catherine Flanagan's statement records that she met Ryan in the druggist's shop at the corner of Burlington Street and saw her purchase poison, light blue in colour. Ryan gave the packet to Flanagan with instructions to give it to Margaret Evans, which she did, and Evans subsequently made her apparently fatal visits to the unfortunate 'Mule' (Charles Mure).

Inspector Boyes[73] tried in vain to trace the purchase of that poison and his only success was to reveal a sale of similar substance to Thomas Stanton, husband of Bridget. He did, however, establish that rat poison was dyed blue.

There is little more to show her involvement with matters criminal but that which does appear is strangely revealing, even in its negative form.

When Ellen Flanagan was giving evidence to the coroner at the inquest into the death of Thomas Higgins,[74] she was asked a question which led her to say that one day, coming home from school, she had left her satchel at Mrs Ryan's house and her little girl Bridget[75] brought it back; an innocent link into which no more can be read other than neighbourly intercourse. However, Ellen then continues in answer to whatever question was next posed:

> I do not remember Mrs Ryan taking some policies away either in a satchel or bag or any other way ... From something Mr Boyes[76] said to me I went to Mrs Ryan and asked her had she got the policies and she said 'No. What have I to do with the policies.' [sic] I do not remember saying 'Yes you did have the policies and sent the bag back by your little girl.'

This line of questioning by the coroner about the school satchel containing insurance policies was not taken further, nor was it pursued at any other venue. If it was an inspired guess on the part of the coroner it was remarkably lucky; one might surmise that Inspector Boyes had coerced Ellen into setting a trap for Mrs Ryan, which might well have succeeded had Ellen not denied the conversation in court. The child was barely fourteen at the time yet clearly in possession of a great deal of information that the police would have dearly loved to extract from her.

It seems unlikely that the advocate was merely embarking on what would now be disallowed as a mere 'fishing expedition' and there is reason to suppose that Ellen knew a great deal about the activities of her mother and aunt. Indeed, in his letter dated 25 February 1884,[77] the prosecuting solicitor for Liverpool, William Marks, told the DPP he thought it likely that Ellen could give 'valuable information' and had reason to believe she would be willing so to do, but only after her mother's execution. Unfortunately no further information can be gleaned about either why he believed that or what happened subsequently.

There is no evidence against Mrs Ryan yet the suspicion of close involvement with Flanagan hangs heavy in the air. According to the *Echo*:[78]

> The police received information yesterday that Flanagan was in a house over a coal yard in St Martin Street. They proceeded to the place and instituted a search but without finding her. According to the information we are in possession of the police searched every room in the house referred to except one at the back where the woman was concealed and when the officers had gone away a female friend who was privy to the concealment remarked "Thanks be to God, Mrs Flanagan ye have luck yet".

This is unlikely to be true for the day in question because Flanagan was with the Booths and did not go out of the house.

This interlinking of the various women demonstrates the close-knit community in which they lived. The Home Office ministers and the Treasury Solicitor both recognised this but perhaps underestimated it, as whatever suspicions neighbours may have had (and according to Maria Hoare's various statements they were many and shrewd) they were remarkably silent when the police were making their enquiries.

It is clear that the two sisters were not the only ones to insure and then kill. They were unfortunate in that clear evidence was found, upon which they were convicted. So far as the other women were concerned there was only circumstantial evidence, in itself cogent, but their salvation lay in the fact that whoever they visited or nursed or co-habited with and poisoned, they were inevitably accompanied by one or other of the sisters. In the rare instances when they were not, then only Flanagan's word accused them and the Home Secretary was loath to grant clemency to Flanagan on the outside chance that her evidence would convince a jury that another person was jointly involved. The jury would have been in an impossible position, convicting one woman and thus inevitably condemning her to death, while accepting Flanagan was also culpable and yet knowing she would not hang as part of her arrangement with the prosecution. Any defence lawyer would lean heavily on the unreliability of Flanagan, clearly fighting for her life.

CHAPTER 8

Conclusions

Oh! God! That bread should be so dear,
And flesh and blood so cheap!

Thomas Hood, *The Song of the Shirt*

BY THE TIME OF THEIR EXECUTION the sisters were portrayed as standing together but isolated. Yet the press hinted, and sometimes even asserted, that the sisters were but part of a ring of like-minded women. It is this aspect which breaks new ground, combining the research of Ellen Ross with that of historians dealing with women's crimes generally. Again, this idea of women banding together to kill has not previously been researched and the established authors do tend to regard murderesses as women standing alone, ostracized by their peers.

There is no doubt that there were many victims not mentioned at the trial who were poisoned for profit, by the sisters and in some cases, their cohorts. There is no doubt about the first group of four, little about the second group of six but considerable dubiety about the final seven. I hope I have been able to demonstrate clearly the network of insuring and killing that existed, and also shown how easy it was to perpetrate these deeds. Much was suspected, probably because it was accepted that murder happened in such situations, and that acceptance itself gives credence to the suspicion. Clearly it was the women who administered the poison to their individual victims, but it is unlikely they would have killed without a financial motive and they would not have been able to kill so easily without easy access to arsenic.

Arguably their task was made easier by the attitude of the insurance companies and the pharmaceutical industry. As shown, the combination of the two laid a straight and well-paved road down which these women and those like them were able to proceed without hindrance. There was serious malpractice which was at best ignored and at worst condoned by the insurers.

To answer the question 'did these two women act alone?,' quite apart from the other women involved, such as Mrs Evans and Mrs Ryan, the wider perspective must be considered.

Without the negligence of the doctors, the easy sale of poisons, the complacency and greed of the insurance companies, the commission paid to agents which encouraged them to seek extra lives to insure, the woman would not have been able to get away with murder. They would have had no financial incentive, no means to procure poison and the doctors would have picked up the first signs of poisoning.

The absence of surprise at what the sisters did speaks volumes. The crimes were condemned, but there are no editorials couched in terms of shocked disbelief at the killings. As Mrs Hoare says on various occasions, 'there was talk'. It was not, then, considered unspeakable. Suspicion of poisoning for life insurance was accepted as a fact of life, whispered about, discussed, fingers were pointed and a slander action taken, but no one, from the Home Secretary and his colleagues[1] to the humblest neighbour in the Liverpool slums, showed any surprise. It was condemned, but there was a weary acceptance that the sisters' actions were not unique. This adds cogency to the theory of community participation. That participation is evident in the way Catherine Flanagan evaded capture for ten days. It is clear that the majority of people who helped her knew her and probably knew why she was running away. The press give the impression that she was effectively shielded and sheltered not only by her friends and acquaintances living within her own community but also with other families, strangers, outside her familiar territory. The police could not penetrate, neither could the press. When she was arrested it seems that it was by luck rather than judgement.

On three nights, Saturday 6, Sunday 7 and Tuesday 9 October, she was drinking in company, in public houses in the area where she had lived for over twenty years. She probably would have been recognised; it is unlikely that she would not have been and the press hinted as much. Her flight and its cause were well publicised and generated much gossip.

This demonstrates the protection she was afforded by her peers and negates any suggestion that they condemned her or her crimes. Despite their evidence no one informed on her; the Ward/McGovern pair said that they did but the veracity of their evidence is cast in doubt by that of Inspector Keighley.

In some ways the sisters were indeed scapegoats but the fact that others escaped retribution does not lessen the sisters' guilt; it merely puts it into perspective, showing that they were two of several, not two alone but part of a very tightly-knit community. The inescapable con-clusion is that Catherine Flanagan and her sister Margaret Higgins were accepted by that community as normal, working-class women, even though part of that normality involved insuring people and then killing them. Others did the same, but escaped justice. The sisters were portrayed as normal women up to their conviction, when their image was manipulated from 'normal' to 'wicked'. There was clearly a sinister side to the community networks and a dark side of poverty, where conscience and caring were subjugated to profit and poison.

As to which sister was the more guilty, the truth will never be known but it does seem probable, in the light of all the evidence, that the two sisters were equally culpable. I cannot believe that Catherine, as she pleaded in her statement, merely involved herself in the insuring of the victims. Even if she did just that, how innocent would she be? Who could pick and insure a person knowing that he or she was going to be killed and then plead a lesser degree of guilt because they did not actually touch the poisoned cup? Strangely, I have always felt that she was not involved in the killing of little Mary Higgins; certainly the stipendiary magistrate declined to commit her for trial on that charge. My reasons are illogical, certainly not borne of legal training, but somehow I feel that if she was willing to admit accepting insurance money gained from the murder of her own son John, why should she quibble about the knowledge of the murder of a barely known child?

All the streets in which the killings took place have been demolished although in some areas the street names still exist but with new properties built after the last war. The archive photographs of their squalor are all that remain to show the grinding poverty and deprivation in which these families lived. Gone too is Dr Whitford's house at 37 Shaw Street, but one section of the street remains and most of the houses in it have been newly cleaned and restored to grace.

Abercrombie Square, where the Stipendiary Magistrate Mr Raffles lived, is now part of the University of Liverpool and its renovated frontage overlooking the central gardens is elegant and peaceful.

St. George's Hall, solidly ostentatious in typical Victorian style, has recently been cleaned and restored. The imposing panelled courtroom where they heard their fate still retains its dark dignity.

This has been a depressing tale of chilling cruelty and calculating greed. But for the tenacity of Patrick Higgins and the open mind of Dr Whitford, the killings would have remained a closely guarded secret among the conspirators. There would have been more victims, I am sure, had the police not been alerted when they were.

It is hoped that the execution of the sisters gave their friends pause for thought but the cynic in me suspects that after a while life – and death – probably carried on as normal.

There are still pockets of research to be explored. I would be interested to know what happened to Mrs Stanton, Mrs Evans, Mrs Ryan and Mrs Begley. I would especially like to know what became of Ellen Flanagan. She was only 14 when her mother hanged and as far as I can ascertain she then lived with her brother Patrick. (He was in prison for something at some stage after his mother's arrest but that is another mystery which I have not been able to solve, despite much research.) Tracing her will not be easy. By the time of the 1891 census she would have been 24 and possibly married or moved. All spellings of Flanagan would have to be checked for her marriage. I may be able to check school records if they survived the second world war bombing of Liverpool, to see if any comments were made, but as she would have left school at 14 it would not assist with her future, only her past. Even if I could find a marriage certificate or other snippets, I would only have bald facts and nothing to tell me what sort of person she became. I did place an advertisement in the Liverpool Family History Magazine about two years ago seeking information from any descendants of the family but had no response.

But I am torn two ways about Ellen. She lived in the house where at least three of those close to her were murdered and her father died too, as did the first Mrs Higgins and Maggie Jennings' mother. Even if those latter three were not murdered (and I suspect they were) she would have been very well acquainted with death for such a young girl. She comes across as a bright girl. Surely she knew? And if she knew, did she accept it as normal? On the other hand she shows a deep bond with her mother whom she may have believed innocent. There is the comment about the police having the intention of speaking to her after the execution. Again I cannot find the police records. If she knew as much as I think, especially if she believed her mother innocent, she would have been a very dangerous girl and I wonder what the other women thought.

Venturing just for a moment into the world of supposition, that last thought might have been the answer to my oft-pondered mystery as to why Catherine Flanagan went to such lengths to distance Mrs Stanton from guilt. I have mentioned this previously when discussing the culpability of the other women. Certainly Bridget Stanton was one of the last of the syndicate to see Catherine before she went into hiding. Is it plausible that they came to an arrangement whereby Mrs Stanton would protect Ellen provided Catherine in turn protected her? When Ellen spent her last few hours alone with her mother in the MacKenzie household, did Catherine tell her to keep Mrs Stanton's involvement quiet at all costs? This would certainly account for this continual distancing of Mrs Stanton, and the Mafia-style protection system thus used does have a plausibility.

Shaw Street.

St George's Hall, Liverpool,
with St John's Church (now demolished) in the background.

Sadly there is no definitive answer to all the speculation about Ellen and I fear her life would have been very difficult. I would be happier to assume her totally innocent but I have a cold feeling about her.

Poor child; in a way, another victim.

Notes and references

Notes to Chapter 1: Pandora's box

1. *Liverpool Echo*, 18 February 1884, p. 3.
2. PRO/21, Memorandum.
3. *The Times*, 4 March 1884, p. 11.
4. *Liverpool Daily Post*, 4 March 1884, p. 3.
5. 1881 census (Liverpool, Lancs, 3598, 127, 32, p. 01234)
6. William Nott-Bower, *Fifty-two Years a Policeman* (London: Edward Arnold, 1926).
7. *Liverpool Echo*, 16 February 1884, p. 3.
8. Report of the Head Constable for Liverpool, Table 1, Indictable Crimes.
9. Period ending 29 September 1884.
10. Table 16, Liverpool Head Constable's report, 1884.
11. Head Constable's report for year ending 1883.

Notes to Chapter 2: Victims

1. As reported *Liverpool Echo*, 16 February 1884, p. 4.
2. PRO, HO 144/126 A 33023/10.
3. PRO, HO 144/126 A 33023/9. Letter dated 22 February 1884. Backsheet bears a note 'Notes to Treasury Solr. 11.3.84'.
4. PRO, HO 144/126 A 33023/21, Memorandum relating to Liverpool Poisoning case and involvement of Friendly Societies, criticising the laxity of the system.
5. PRO, A33023/12.
6. Wrote to *The Lancet*, 4 March 1884.
7. PRO/13.
8. *Liverpool Daily Post*, 15 February 1884, p. 7.
9. Certificate of marriage, see appendix 4. Both then living with Catherine Flanagan at 31 Blewnheim Street.
10. COR/TH various.
11. COR/TH E. Lawton.
12. COR/TH Manville and CTTL/TH Manville.
13. PRO, HO ETC /10.
14. COR/TH Lawton.
15. *Liverpool Daily Post*, 15 February 1884, p. 7., quoting the opening speech for the prosecution by Mr J. B. Aspinall, QC, Recorder of Liverpool.
16. COR/TH Whitford & CTTLE /TH Whitford.
17. CTTL/TH W. Bennett, exhibit WB 1.
18. COR/TH Manville.
19. COR/TH Griffiths.
20. COR/TH Cartwright.
21. Ibid., exhibit WJC 1.
22. Ibid., exhibit WJC 2.
23. COR/TH Williams.
24. COR/TH Finnegan.
25. *Liverpool Daily Post*, 16 February 1884, p. 7.
26. COR/TH Finegan.
27. COR/TH Finegan.
28. CTTL/TH Marshall, exhibit AM 1.
29. CTTL/TH Bennett.
30. CTTCL/TH Bennett, exhibit DB 1.
31. CTTL/TH Bennett, exhibit DB 5.

32. CTTL/TH Bennett, exhibit DB 2.
33. CTTL/TH John Bowles, exhibit JB 1.
34. CTTL/TH F. D. Bowles.
35. CTTL/TH F. D. Bowles. Form on back of exhibit JB 1 and dated 22 March 1883.
36. CTTL/TH F. D. Bowles policy exhibited as FDB 1.
37. CTTL/TH, exhibit JB 1.
38. *Liverpool Echo*, Saturday 15 December 1883, p. 4.
39. Exhibit JDB 3.
40. Exhibit JDB 4.
41. COR/TH Jones.
42. CTTL/TH, RJ 1.
43. CTTL/TH, Indictment.
44. CTTL/TH, P. Higgins.
45. *Liverpool Echo*, 13 December 1883, p. 4. quoting opening speech for prosecution by Mr Marks (Prosecuting Solicitor for Liverpool) at committal proceedings in respect of murder of Thomas Higgins.
46. The 1881 census gives his age as 42 in April 1881.
47. CTTL/TH, P. Higgins.
48. COR/TH, P. Higgins.
49. CTTL/TH, P. Higgins.
50. COR/TH, P. Higgins.
51. CTTL/TH, Dr Whitford.
52. COR/TH, P. Higgins.
53. St Catherine's Index, ref. 8b 386; see also copy marriage certificate.
54. *The Lancet*, 1884, vol. 1, p. 420, and confirms her date of death as 29 November 1882.
55. CTTL/MH, P. Jennings.
56. COR/TH, P. Higgins.
57. Public Grave SV 944, Ford Cemetery.
58. CTTL/TH, J. Williams.
59. PRO, HO 144/126 A 33023/3, Letter 8 January 1884 Marks, Prosecuting Solicitor to Home Secretary requesting permission to exhume her body. Order duly made the next day.
60. Frederick Walter Lowndes, surgeon to the Liverpool City Police residing at 40 Knight Street, Liverpool.
61. CTTL/MH Lowndes.
62. CTTL/MH Whitford, residing at 37 Shaw Street, Liverpool.
63. CTTL/MH Davies.
64. PRO, 74478 H.O. 144/126 A33023/10 PRO/10.
65. CTTL/MH.
66. She is listed in the 1881 census as living at 142 Blenheim Street, aged 15, Domestic Servant born Liverpool. Also in the same house are Catherine Flanagan (head of household), Margaret (May) Higgins (then Thompson), Patrick Jennings, Ellen Flanagan, Patrick Flanagan and another two male lodgers. Buried Ford, 28 January 1883, grave SV999 (Public Grave).
67. CTTL/MJ, P. Jennings.
68. CTTL/MJ, P. Jennings.
69. CTTL/MJ, Dr Rafter, John Patrick Rafter Surgeon, 383 Fountains Road.
70. CTTL/MJ, Rafter, January 12, 15, 17, 20, 22, 24.
71. CTTL/MJ, P. Jennings.
72. CTTL/MJ, Rafter.
73. Wife of Stephen Wharton, 11 Skirving Street, formerly living in cellar under 5 Skirving Street. CTTL/MJ Wharton.
74. CTTL/MJ, P. Jennings.
75. CTTL/MJ, Wharton.
76. COR/MJ, P. Jennings the younger.
77. CTTL/MJ, P. Jennings.
78. On 21 June 1882, for the sum of £18. CTTL/MJ, Griffiths. COR/TH Cartwright.
79. CTTL/MJ, G. Griffiths.
80. CTTL/MJ, W. J. Cartwright, exhibit WJC 3.
81. CTTL/MJ, P. Dolan, exhibit PD 1.
82. CTTL/MJ, P. Dolan, exhibit PD 1.
83. CTTL/MJ, W. J. Cartwright, exhibit WJC 4.
84. *The Liverpool Echo*, 29 December 1883, p. 4.
85. COR/MJ, P. Higgins.
86. COR/MJ, P. Jennings the younger.
87. COR/MJ, A. Wharton.
88. COR/MJ, P. Jennings. Grave SV999 per Ford Cemetery Liverpool Archdiocesan Cemetery Board Records.
89. PRO/1, Letter Marks to Home Secretary (Sir William Harcourt), 3 November 1883. Second letter dated

5 November 1883 from Marks to Lushington (Assistant Secretary, Home Office) acknowledging receipt of exhumation order. In PRO/2.
90. Per Ford Cemetery records.
91. COR/MJ, Lowndes.
92. COR/MJ, Davies, Edward Davies, Fellow of the Chemical Society of London and and Fellow of the Institute of Chemistry. Analytical and Consulting Chemist at the Royal Institution in Liverpool.
93. CTTL/MJ 7 TH. Campbell Brown.
94. CTTL/MJ Lowndes.
95. CTTL/MJ Edward Davies.
96. PRO/10. Also statement is referred to in letter dated 1 March 1884 from Treasury Solicitor (Cuffe) to Sir A. F. O'Liddell at Home Office, PRO/17.
97. Per Maria Hoare, p. 4, Echo, 19 October 1883: 'and when the girl Jennings was buried expressions were used that there had been poisoning going on ...'.
98. COR/TH, J. Williams.
99. COR/MJ, W. Howley.
100. COR/MJ, J. Smith.
101. COR/MJ, P. Dolan.
102. Other references to Maggie; COR and CTTL papers COR/TH. She died in Skirving Street per Ellen F statement CTTL/TH 137–146, 147–151 Dr, 152 –166, 171–182, 183, 184, 185/7, 188 CTTL/MJ general p. 47 note Whitehead says Mrs Wharton was with Pat Jennings. However, p. 7 Jennings says it was CF, JF and EF ('all four'); p. 47. A 'Aunt' on death certificate.
103. PRO/3, letter Marks to Harcourt.
104. Body was later re-interred in the same public grave, SV 464 per Ford.
105. Liverpool Echo, 19 October 1883, p. 4.
106. CTTL/JF, Hoare.
107. CTTL/MJ, Wharton.
108. See certificate.
109. CTTL/JF, Whitford.
110. CTTL/JF, Lowndes.
111. CTTL/JF, Davies.
112. CTTL/JF.
113. Liverpool Daily Post, Saturday 16 February 1884, p. 7.
114. Liverpool Echo, 19 October 1883, p. 4.
115. PRO/10.
116. CTTL/JF, J. M. Gwynne.
117. CTTL/JF, A. Marshall.
118. CTTL/JF, Mr Bond and J. M. Gwynne.
119. CTTL/JF, D. Hoolihan.
120. Hoolihan states original sum assured unknown.
121. CTTL/JF, D. Hoolihan.
122. CTTL/JF, Frances Dominic Bowles.
123. CTTL/JF, W. H. Hivey.
124. CTTL/JF, John Thompson Clarke.
125. CTTL/JF, George Griffiths.
126. John Flanagan died on 7 December 1880.
127. Other references to John Flanagan found in CTTL/JF, and PRO/17.
128. PRO, HO 144/126 A 33023/6 letter 25 February 1884, Prosecuting Solicitor Liverpool to DPP.
129. PRO, HO 144/126 A 33023/10.
130. PRO, HO 144/126 A33023/10.
131. Per Ford Cemetery Records.
132. PRO, 74478 HO 144/126 A33023/6 letter W. W. Marks (Prosecuting Solicitor Liverpool) to DPP dated 25 February 1884.
133. A 33023/10, Flanagan's statement.
134. See certificate.
135. A33023/17 letter H. Cuffe (Treasury Solicitor), to Sir A. F. O'Liddell at Home Office dated 1 March 1884.
136. Liverpool Echo, 19 October 1883, p. 4.
137. Per Ford.
138. See certificate.
139. A33023/10 Flanagan's statement.
140. A33023/10, Flanagan's statement.
141. PRO/6.
142. Per Ford.
143. A33023/17, letter Treasury Solicitor to O'Liddell at Home Office dated 1 March 1884.
144. CTTL/JF 26/27.
145. PRO/17.
146. Per Ford.
147. PRO/10.
148. PRO/17 P45
149. PRO/10.

150. 1881 census. Shown as 34 St Martin Street, Owen Dock, Labourer aged 40, Bridget aged 42, both born in Ireland.
151. PRO/10.
152. Inspector Stephen Boyes, 1881 census, p. 06482 aged 38, born Scotland.
153. PRO/17, report of Inspector Boyes and letter Treasury to Home Office both same file.
154. PRO/17.
155. PRO/17, letter Treasury Solicitor to HO.
156. PRO/17, statement to Inspector Boyes.
157. *Liverpool Echo*, 19 October 1883 p. 4. She gives the address as 33 St Martin Street, with the Begleys.
158. Other reference to Godfrey at PRO/6.
159. PRO/17, letter treasury to HO.
160. Per Ford.
161. Margaret Evans 1881 census possible trace p. 007477 at 93 Prince Edwin Street, PRO/10 Flanagan's statement refers to her as a fishwoman living in Blenheim Street.
162. PRO/17, report of Inspector Boyes.
163. PRO/10, Flanagan's statement.
164. PRO/17, Maria Hoare's statement.
165. Other references to Neillan PRO/6 and /17, general discussion Evans/Higgins culpability, Flanagan 'does not profess to know anything'.
166. PRO/6.
167. PRO/17.
168. PRO/17, died 14 March 1883.
169. PRO/17, Inspector Boyes' report.
170. PRO/10, Flanagan's statement.
171. 1881 census p. 01189 Catherine Ryan aged 35, wife of Martin, aged 40, a dock labourer, both born Ireland, with five children and three lodgers at 32 St Martin Street, next to Mrs Bridget Begley at 34.
172. Possible census trace 1881 p. 07477

at 93 Prince Edwin Street aged 54, born Liverpool, a shopkeeper, married. Note next door is a fishmonger and Flanagan describes Evans as a fishwife.
173. PRO/10, Flanagan's statement.
174. PRO/17, Inspector Boyes' report.
175. PRO/17, H. Cuffe, Treasury Solicitor. Report in letter dated dated 1 March 1884 to Home Office relating to visit to Liverpool.
176. PRO/17.
177. PRO/17, Treasury Solicitor's report.
178. PRO/17, Inspector Boyes' report dated 18 Febrary 1884.
179. PRO/17, Inspector Boyes' report.
180. Other references to Mure, PRO/6.
181. PRO/17, Inspector Boyes' report.
182. *Liverpool Echo*, 18 February 1884.
183. COR/MJ, P. Jennings the elder.
184. CTTL/MJ, P. Jennings the elder.
185. *Liverpool Echo*, 11 October 1883 p. 4.
186. *Liverpool Daily Post*, 12 October 1883.
187. *Liverpool Echo*, 19 October 1883, p. 4.
188. Ibid., 19 October 1883, p. 4.
189. CTTL/JFF, Maria Hoare.
190. *Liverpool Echo*, 19 October 1883, p. 4.
191. CTTL/JF.
192. *Liverpool Echo*, 19 October 1883, p. 4.
193. COR/JF, M. Hoare.
194. *Liverpool Echo*, 19 October 1883, p. 4.
195. Per Ford Cemetery Records.
196. *Liverpool Echo*, 19 October 1883, p. 4.
197. Census, 1871, possible trace 4 House, 12 Court, 22 St Martin Street aged 40, widow, Hawker, born Ireland also Elizabeth Evans aged 6 years, born Lancs.
198. CTTL/JF, Maria Hoare.
199. *Liverpool Echo*, 19 October 1883, p. 4.
200. COR/TH, Patrick Higgins.
201. *Liverpool Daily Post*, 15 February 1884, p. 7.

Notes to Chapter 3: Murderesses

1. *Liverpool Daily Post*, 18 February 1884, p. 5.
2. COR/MJ, P. Dolan, Royal Liver Insurance Company.
3. *Liverpool Daily Post*, 17 October 1883.
4. Kanya-Forstner, M., 'The Politics of Survival: Irish Women in Outcast Liverpool, 1850–1890', PhD Thesis, Liverpool, 1997, p. 14.
5. Advertisements appearing in various editions of the *Liverpool Echo* during October 1883.
6. *Liverpool Daily Post*, 18 February 1884, p. 5.
7. *Liverpool Echo*, 19 October 1883, p. 4.
8. COR/JF, M. Hoare.
9. *Liverpool Echo*, 16 October 1883, p. 3.
10. See chapter 4 dealing with her flight.
11. *Liverpool Echo*, 17 October 1883, p. 4.
12. *Liverpool Echo*, 17 October 1883, p. 4.
13. *Liverpool Echo*, 16 October 1883, p. 3.
14. *Liverpool Daily Post*, 4 March 1884, p. 3.
15. *Liverpool Echo*, 17 October 1883, p. 4.
16. Ellen Ross, 'Survival Networks: women's neighbourhood sharing in London before World War One' *History Workshop Journal*, 15 (1983).
17. *Liverpool Daily Post*, 15 February 1884, p. 7.
18. 16 February 1884 both *Liverpool Echo* p. 3. and *Liverpool Daily Post*, p. 3.
19. *Liverpool Echo*, 17 October 1883, p. 4.
20. *Liverpool Daily Post*, 17 October 1883.
21. *Liverpool Echo*, 10 October 1883, p. 4.
22. *Liverpool Daily Post*, 15 October 1883.
23. *Liverpool Echo*, 13 October 1883, p. 4.
24. *Liverpool Echo*, 16 October 1883, p. 3.
25. *Liverpool Echo*, 15 October 1883, p. 3.
26. *Liverpool Daily Post*, 12 October 1883.
27. *Liverpool Echo*, 16 October 1883, p. 2.
28. *Liverpool Echo*, 13 December 1883, p. 4.
29. *Liverpool Echo*, 11 October 1883, p. 4.
30. *Liverpool Echo*, 12 October 1883, p. 4.

Notes to Chapter 4: Catherine's last days of freedom

1. *Liverpool Echo*, 14 February 1884 p. 4.
2. *Liverpool Echo*, 16 February 1884 p. 4.
3. *Liverpool Daily Post*, 18 February 1884. The prosecution's closing speech had lasted nearly one hour and the judge was to take two and a half hours.
4. *Liverpool Echo*, 11 October 1883, p. 4.
5. All references are to COR/TH or CTTL/TH where the evidence is virtually the same, except where otherwise stated. The evidence is taken from the statement of the person assisting or the householder referred to.
6. Spelling varies in court papers, CTTL/TH spelt MacKenzie, COR/TH spelt McKenzie.
7. According to *Liverpool Daily Post*, 17 October 1883.
8. *Liverpool Daily Post*, 17 October 1883.
9. *Liverpool Daily Post*, 17 October 1883.
10. CTTL/TH, Mrs MacKenzie.
11. COR/TH, Mrs MacKenzie.
12. *Liverpool Daily Post*, 17 October 1883.
13. *Liverpool Daily Post*, 17 October 1883.
14. *Liverpool Daily Post*, 15 October 1883.
15. Ross, Ellen, 'Survival Networks: women's neighbourhood sharing in London before World War one.' *History Workshop*, vol. 15 (Oxford: Oxford University Press, 1983).
16. *Liverpool Daily Post*, 17 October 1883.
17. *Liverpool Echo*, 16 February 1884.
18. According to *Liverpool Daily Post*, 17 October 1883.
19. *Liverpool Echo*, 16 February 1884, p. 4.

20. *Liverpool Daily Post*, 17 October 1883; also *Liverpool Echo*, 17 October 1883, p. 4.
21. *Liverpool Daily Post*, 17 October 1883.
22. *Liverpool Daily Post*, 17 October 1883.
23. This is virtually the same as evidence given at the committal and coroner's court but at the committal it included the phrase 'she's still at large'.
24. CTTL/TH, J. MacKenzie.
25. *Liverpool Daily Post*, 17 October 1883.
26. *Liverpool Daily Post*, 17 October 1883.
27. According to *Liverpool Echo*, 15 December 1883, he is a labourer living at 35 Blundell Street. This is adjacent to Cornwallis Street where the Mackenzies lived. The only trace of a Thomas Barrett in Liverpool in the 1881 census surname index for Lancashire is a 24-year-old bachelor, occupation dock labourer, the same as James MacKenzie.
28. *Liverpool Daily Post*, 17 October 1883.
29. *Liverpool Daily Post*, 17 October 1883.
30. *Liverpool Echo*, 16 February 1884, p. 4.
31. Mrs Booth gave evidence to the coroner and at the committal.
32. *Liverpool Daily Post*, 17 October 1883.
33. *Liverpool Echo*, Saturday 13 October 1883, p. 4.
34. *Liverpool Echo*, Monday 15 October 1883, p. 3.
35. *Liverpool Echo*, 15 October 1883, p. 3.
36. *Liverpool Echo*, Saturday 13 October 1883, p. 4.
37. *Liverpool Echo*, 13 October 1883, p. 4. Also says her husband left her and went to America, refers to Catherine as the mother of Margaret Higgins, whereas they were sisters. States Thomas and Margaret Higgins were married nine years ago whereas they had been married less than a year.
38. *Liverpool Echo*, 16 February 1883, p. 4.
39. *Liverpool Echo*, 13 October 1883, p. 3.
40. *Liverpool Echo*, 12 October 1883, p. 4.
41. *Liverpool Daily Post*, 17 October 1883.
42. *Liverpool Echo*, 28 December 1883, p. 4.
43. COR/TH, McGovern.
44. *Liverpool Daily Post*, 17 October 1883.
45. *Liverpool Echo*, 28 December 1883, p. 4.
46. 1881 census details Aspinall. Clarke Aspinall was a solicitor and Liverpool City Coroner. He is listed in the 1881 census as 53, born Liverpool, living at Laurel Bank, Bebington. He was the brother of John Bridge Aspinall, QC, the Recorder of Liverpool who prosecuted at the trial.
47. *Liverpool Daily Post*, 15 February 1884, p. 7.
48. *Liverpool Echo*, 16 February 1884, p. 4.
49. *Liverpool Echo*, 16 October 1883, p. 3.
50. *Liverpool Echo*, 16 October 1883, p. 3.
51. *Liverpool Echo*, 16 October 1883. p. 3.
52. *Liverpool Echo*, 16 February 1884.
53. COR/TH, Mr MacKenzie.
54. CTTL/TH, Mr MacKenzie.

Notes to Chapter 5: Courtroom and scaffold

1. *Liverpool Echo*, 19 October 1883, p. 3.
2. *Liverpool Echo*, 19 October 1883, p. 4.
3. *Liverpool Daily Post*, 16 February 1884, p. 7.
4. *Liverpool Echo*, 15 February 1884, p. 3.
5. *Liverpool Daily Post*, 15 February 1884, p. 5.
6. *Liverpool Echo*, 16 February 1884, p. 3.
7. *Liverpool Daily Post*, 15 February 1884, p. 7.
8. *Liverpool Echo*, 3 March 1884, p. 4. and *Liverpool Daily Post* same date, both virtually the same wording.
9. *Liverpool Echo*, 3 March 1884, p. 4.
10. *The Times*, 12 June 2001, pp. 1, 4, 5.

11. *The Times*, 4 March 1884, p. 11.
12. *Liverpool Daily Post*, 3 March 1884, p. 3, and the *Echo*, same date, p. 4.
13. *Liverpool Daily Post*, 18 February 1884, p. 5.
14. *Liverpool Echo*, 18 February 1884, p. 3.

Notes to Chapter 6: Collusion and blind eyes

1. Knelman, Judith, *Twisting in the Wind: The Murderess and the English Press* (Toronto: University of Toronto Press, 1998).
2. *Liverpool Echo*, 29 December 1883, p. 4.
3. CTTL/TH, Whitford. He also made the point clear in his article in *The Lancet*, vol. 1, 1884, p. 419.
4. *Liverpool Echo*, 14 February 1884, p. 4.
5. *The Lancet*, vol. 1, 1884, pp. 419–21.
6. *Liverpool Echo*, 15 December 1883, p. 4.
7. *The Lancet*, vol. 1, 1884, p. 351.
8. *Liverpool Echo*, 11 October 1883, p. 4.
9. CTTL/JF, Whitford.
10. CTTL/JF, Lowndes.
11. *The Times*, 6 September 1849, p. 5.
12. A short biographical article appears in *The Times*, 2, 25 June 2001, p. 5.
13. Knelman, *Twisting in the Wind*, pp. 67–8.
14. *The Lancet*, vol. 1, 1884, p. 402.
15. H.O. file, PRO HO144/126 A33023/21.
16. *The Lancet*, vol. 1, 1884, p. 401.
17. *Liverpool Daily Post*, 17 October 1883.
18. *Liverpool Echo*, 18 February 1884, p. 3.
19. CTTL/TH, D. C. Musgrave.
20. CTTL/TH, Davies.
21. A pocket on tape tied around the waist. Phillis Cunnington and Catherine Lucas, *Occupational Costume in England from the Eleventh Century to 1914* (London: Black, 1967).
22. CTTL/TH, Inspector Maxwell.
23. CTTL/TH, Davies.
24. *Liverpool Daily Post*, 16 February 1884, p. 7.
25. *Liverpool Echo*, 16 February 1884, p. 4.
26. PRO/10, Letter from Neale to DPP, 22 February 1884.
27. *Liverpool Daily Post*, 15 February 1884, p. 7.
28. 'To Hell with the clubs etc.' is a direct quote from the statement of an agent from the Mr R. Jones given at the coroner's inquest into Thomas Higgins' death.
29. H.O. file, PRO HO144/126 A33023/21.
30. *Liverpool Daily Post*, 18 February 1884, p. 5.
31. *Liverpool Echo*, 15 October 1883, p. 3. quoting the *Manchester Examiner*.
32. *Liverpool Daily Post*, 18 February 1884, p. 5.
33. *Liverpool Daily Post*, 12 October 1883.
34. *Liverpool Daily Post*, 15 October 1883.'Catherine Flanagan who is suspected of having first entered people in burial clubs and friendly societies and afterwards poisoned them for the insurance money.'
35. *Liverpool Echo*, 13 October 1883, p. 4.
36. John Bridge Aspinall.
37. *Liverpool Daily Post*, 15 February 1884, p. 7.
38. Chadwick: Interment in Towns. Royal Commission Report 1843 (509) XII 395, pp. 54–64.
39. Friendly Societies Select Committee Report 1889 (304) X. 413.
40. J. D. J. Havard *The Detection of Secret Homicide* (London, 1960).
41. F. W. Lowndes, *Reasons why the Office of Coroner should be held by a Member of the Medical Profession* (London, 1892).
42. Glasgow, Gordon, 'Clarke Aspinall: Liverpool Borough Coroner', *Lancashire History Quarterly*, vol. 3, Issue No. 1, March 1999.
43. Glasgow, Gordon, 'Clarke Aspinall: Liverpool Borough Coroner,' *Lancashire History Quarterly*, vol. 3, Issue No. 1, March 1999.

Quoting Reports from Commission on Friendly and Benefit Burial Societies. vol. XXIII, Part 1. Fourth report Appendix VII. p. 93.

44. For examples see: CTTL/TH exhibit RJ1 Richard Jones. Agent for Royal Liver Friendly Society: CTTL/TH Finegan (claim form): CTTL/TH D. Barr exhibit DB 2: COR/TH Bennett.

45. F. D. Bowles giving evidence at the committal proceedings relating to Thomas Higgins reported in *Liverpool Echo*, 15 December 1883, p. 4.

46. CTTL/TH, exhibit RJ 1, Richard Jones.

47. CTTL/TH, Finegan.

48. *Liverpool Echo*, 15 February 1884, p. 4.

49. *Liverpool Echo*, 15 February 1884, p. 4.

50. *Liverpool Echo*, 15 February 1884, p. 4. again quoting from evidence given at trial.

51. It is not clear which prisoner he meant.

52. Ibid., 16 February 1884, p. 7.

53. Also reported in *Liverpool Daily Post*, 16 February 1884, p. 7, naming Mr Finegan.

54. Ibid.

55. Ibid.

56. *Liverpool Echo*, 16 February 1884, p. 4, reporting closing speeches.

57. *Liverpool Echo*, 16 February 1884, p. 4, reporting closing speeches.

58. *Liverpool Daily Post*, 16 February 1884, p. 7.

59. *Liverpool Echo*, 18 February 1994, p. 3.

60. *Liverpool Daily Post*, 18 February 1884, p. 5.

61. *The Lancet*, vol. 1, 1884, p. 352.

62. *The Lancet*, vol. 1, 1884, p. 403.

63. Referring to the Shipman case.

64. PRO/17 letter treasury to Liddell at Home Office, 1 March 1884.

65. *Liverpool Echo*, 12 October 1883, p. 4.

66. 'To Hell with the clubs etc.' is a direct quote from the statement of an agent from the Mr R. Jones given at the Coroner's inquest into Thomas Higgins' death.

67. Letter Treasury to Liddell, 1 March 1884, PRO/17.

68. PRO/21, memorandum with results of this investigation. Gives many detailed examples of laxity of insurance rules.

Notes to Chapter 7: The Poisoning Syndicate

1. PRO/6, LETTER Marks (Prosecuting Solicitor Liverpool) to DPP.

2. PRO/10, letter H. F. Neale to DPP, dated 22 February 1884 enclosing statement of Catherine Flanagan which he says is written before her conviction.

3. PRO/17, letter Treasury Solicitor to Home Office dated 1 March 1884.

4. *Liverpool Echo*, 18 February 1884, p. 4.

5. PRO, HO 144/126 A33023/10. Statement of Catherine Flanagan.

6. Census 1871 possible trace 4 House, 12 Court, 22 St Martin Street, aged 40, widow, Hawker, born Ireland also Elizabeth Evans aged 6 years, born Lancs.

7. PRO/17, Treasury Solicitor to Sir A. F. O. Liddell, Home Office, dated 1 March 1884.

8. PRO/10 Statement of Catherine Flanagan.

9. PRO/17, Inspector Boyes report.

10. PRO/17, letter, 1 March, Treasury to Home Office.

11. PRO file generally.

12. PRO/10, Statement of Catherine Flanagan.

13. PRO/17, Inspector Boyes' report.

14. PRO/17, Statement of Maria Hoare.

15. CTTL/MJ, John Smith statement.

16. CTTL/MJ, Statement of John Smith and exhibit JS 2.

17. PRO/17, Inspector Boyes' report.

18. PRO/10, Statement of Catherine Flanagan.

19. *Liverpool Echo*, 19 October 1883, p. 4. per statement of Maria Hoare.

20. Ross, Ellen, 'Survival Networks: women's neighbourhood sharing in London before World War One', *History Workshop*, vol. 15. (Oxford: Oxford University Press, 1983).

21. Other references to Evans: PRO/6, PRO/17.

22. 1881 census, Lancashire, Liverpool 35 98 127 32, p. 01234.

23. PRO/17 letter Treasury Solicitor to Liddell at Home Office. 1 March 1884.

24. PRO/10, Statement of Catherine Flanagan.

25. COR/TH Finegan. CTTL/TH Cartwright, exhibit WJC/1. CTTL/ TH, A. Marshall, exhibit AM4.

26. COR/TH, Finegan.

27. CTTL/TH, Finegan.

28. COR/TH, Finegan.

29. CTTL/TH Cartwright, exhibit WJC/1.

30. CTTL/TH, A. Marshall, exhibit AM 4.

31. PRO/10, Statement of Catherine Flanagan.

32. PRO/17, Statement of Maria Hoare.

33. COR/MJ, and CTTL/TH, Howley.

34. CTTL/TH, and CTTL/MH, Howley.

35. COR/MJ, J. Smith.

36. PRO/17 Report of Inspector Boyes.

37. PRO/ 17. p. 59.

38. *Liverpool Echo*, 19 October 1883, p. 4.

39. Marriage Certificate of Margaret Thompson to Thomas Higgins.

40. COR/TH. Ellen Flanagan.

41. COR/TH Finegan.

42. *Liverpool Echo*, 13 October 1883, p. 4.

43. COR/TH, Finegan.

44. CTTL/TH, Finegan.

45. COR/TH, Finegan.

46. COR/TH, Finegan.

47. PRO/21, Memorandum relating to Insurance.

48. CTTL/TH, Cartwright.

49. CTTL/TH, Cartwright, exhibit WJC1.

50. COR/TH, Cartwright.

51. *Liverpool Daily Post*, 16 February 1884, p. 7.

52. *Liverpool Echo*, 19 October 1883, p. 4.

53. Other references; PRO/21 and CTTL/TH Finegan.

54. PRO/10, Statement of Catherine Flanagan.

55. *Liverpool Echo*, 19 October 1883, p. 4.

56. PRO/17.

57. PRO/17.

58. *Liverpool Echo*, 19 October 1883, p. 4.

59. 1871 census Bridget Begley lived at No. 4 house, 12 Court, 22 St Martin Street.

60. 1881 census Liverpool, Lancs, 3598.78.3. p. 01189 Begley. She is listed as aged 42 with husband Owen aged 40 a dock labourer. Both born Ireland with three sons, born Liverpool.

61. PRO/10. Statement of Catherine Flanagan.

62. *Liverpool Echo*, 19 October 1883, p. 4.

63. PRO/17, Statement of Maria Hoare.

64. PRO/17, report of Inspector Boyes.

65. PRO/17, letter 1 March 1884, Treasury to Liddell.

66. The death certificate shows Mrs Begley as 'cousin' of the deceased and that she was present at the death, neither fact being true.

67. PRO/17, Statement of Maria Hoare.

68. 1881 census Liverpol, Lancs, 3599.134.87. p. 01369.

69. PRO/17. P 58.

70. PRO/17. Letter Treasury Solicitor to Home Office, 1 March 1884.

71. PRO/10. Statement of Catherine Flanagan.

72. 1881 census Liverpool, Lancs, 3598.78.3. p. 01189. Her age is given as 35, which does not correlate to the previous census return, but her husband has correctly aged ten years. They are listed with five children and three lodgers.

73. PRO/17.

74. COR/TH, E. Flanagan.

75. Census 1881 Liverpool, Lancs, 3598.78.3. p. 01189, gives her age as 7.

76. Inspector Boyes, the police officer investigating the murder.

77. PRO/6 Letter, Marks (Prosecuting
Solicitor Liverpool) to DPP.

78. *Liverpool Echo*, 13 October 1883,
p. 4.

Note to Chapter 8: Conclusions

1. PRO/21, Memorandum.

Photograph credits

The marriage and death certificates reproduced in the book are from the Office for National Statistics © Crown copyright, reproduced with the permission of the Controller of HMSO and Queen's Printer for Scotland

Page 6: Liverpool Record Office, Liverpool Libraries, Blenheim Street, 1971, reference 352 HOU 139/9

Page 7: reproduced from *Fifty-Two Years a Policeman* by William Nott-Bower (Edward Arnold, 1926)

Page 8: image of Margaret Higgins reproduced by permission of Madame Tussaud's, London

Pages 20–1: Liverpool Record Office, Liverpool Libraries, No. 2 Court, Silvester Street, July 1913, reference 352 82/19

Page 38: Insurance Proposal Form reproduced by permission of The National Archives

Page 65: author's collection

Page 89: Liverpool Record Office, Liverpool Libraries, Clarke Aspinall from H920 ASP (Lewin, W., *Clarke Aspinall: a Biography*, 1893)

Page 91: *Illustrated Police News*, 1884, with kind permission of The British Library

Page 94: author's collection

Page 96: Judge Mr Justice Butt, from *The Graphic*, 1892

Page 99: *Illustrated Police News*, 1884, with kind permission of The British Library

Page 100: Liverpool Record Office, Liverpool Libraries, print of Kirkdale Gaol print, 1832 (from *Lancashire Illustrated*)

Page 102: Execution certificate, by permission of the National Archives

Page 103: *Illustrated Police News*, 1884, with kind permission of The British Library

Page 139: author's collection

Page 140: Liverpool Record Office, Liverpool Libraries, St George's Hall exterior *c*.1861, watercolour by W Herdman

Bibliography

Primary sources

Report of the Police Establishment and the State of Crime for year ending 29 September 1884 Watch Committee for the City of Liverpool (Liverpool: Greenwood, 1884).

Similarly for 1882, 1883, 1885, 1886. The reports for the last two years were published by A Russell, Son & Bayley, Liverpool.

Reg. *v.* Flanagan and Higgins (1884) (15 Cox C.C. 403).

Law Society Personal files relating to Francis Quelch and Henry Fitzwilliam Neale.

Lincoln's Inn Library Archives relating to William Robert McConnell and Henry Gordon Shee and Sir Charles Parker Butt.

Marriage Certificate of Thomas Higgins and Margaret Thompson, 28 October 1882.

Death certificates of Mary Donnelly, Stephen Flannigan, Mary Higgins, Mary Flanagan, Bridget Jennings, John Flanagan Snr., John Flannigan Jnr.

Public Record Office, Home Office, HO 144/126/A33023 relating to Flanagan and Higgins.

Public Record Office, Home Office, HO 144/289/B830 relating to E. Berry.

Public Record Office, ASSI 52/6 1884 relating to coroner's inquests, committal proceedings for Flanagan and Higgins.

1871 and 1881 Census Returns for Liverpool.

Correspondence between Henry Pearson, Pearson Collinson, Funeral Directors, Liverpool, and self. September 2000.

Correspondence between Rosy Canter, Archivist, Madame Tussauds, London and self between July 2000 and September 2001.

Liverpool Daily Post, October 1883 to March 1884, various dates.

Liverpool Echo, October 1883 to March 1884, various dates.

The Times, March 1884.

The Law Times, 29 December 1906, vol. 122; 20 February 1909, vol. 126.

The Law Journal, 29 December 1906, vol. 41. 20 February 1909, vol.44.

The Graphic, 4 June 1892.

Records of the Catholic Cemeteries Board, Archdiocese of Liverpool.

1874 Royal Commission on Burial Societies; evidence given by C. Aspinall.

Reports from Commission on Friendly and Benefit Burial Societies. vol. XXIII, Part 1. Fourth report Appendix VII.

Chadwick: Interment in Towns. Royal Commission Report 1843(509) XII 395.

Friendly Societies Select Committee Report 1899 (304) X413.

Lowndes, F.W.: Reasons why the Office of Coroner should be held by a Member of the Medical Profession. London 1892.

Secondary Sources

Allan, Adrian R. *The Building of Abercrombie Square* (Liverpool: Liverpool University, 1986).

Ackroyd, Peter, 'Ritual of Death', *The Times 2*, 4 October 2000, pp. 3–4.

Altick, Richard D., *Victorian Studies in Scarlet* (London: Dent, 1972).

Anon, 'The Poison Shop', from *Punch*, published in *The Times*, 6 September 1849, p. 5.

Burney, Ian A., 'A Poisoning of No Substance: The Trials of Medico-Legal Proof in Mid-Victorian England', *Journal of British Studies* 38, January 1999), pp. 59–92.

Chinn, C., *They Worked all their Lives: Women of the Urban Poor in England 1880–1939* (Manchester: Manchester University Press, 1988).

Chadwick, Roger, *Bureaucratic Mercy: The Home Office and the Treatment of Capital Cases in Victorian Britain* (New York: Garland, Modern European History Series, 1992).

Clay, John, *Burial Clubs and Infanticide in England: A Letter to W.Brown Esq., M.P.* (Preston: 1884).

Cockerell, H.A.L., and Green, Edwin, *The British Insurance Business 1547–1970* (London: Heinemann, 1976).

Cooke, T., *Scotland Road: The Old Neighbourhood* (Birkenhead: Countyvise, 1987).

Cunnington, Phillis and Lucas, Catherine, *Occupational Costume in England: From the Eleventh Century to 1914* (London: Adam & Charles Black, 1967).

Davies, Andrew, 'These viragos are no less cruel than the lads', *Brit. J. Criminology*, 39, No.1. Special Issue, 1999.

Dawson, Jill, Fred and Edie (London: Sceptre, 2000).

Emsley, Clive, *Crime and Society in England 1750–1900*, 2nd edn (London: Longman, 1996).

Emmerichs, Mary Beth Wasserlein, 'Trials of Women for Homicide in Nineteenth-Century England' *Woman & Criminal Justice*, 5 (1) 1993.

Gattrell, V.A.C. and Hadden, T.S., 'Criminal statistics and their interpretation', *Nineteenth-century Society*, edited by E.A.Wrigley, (Cambridge: Cambridge University Press, 1972).

Gatrell, V.A.C., *The Hanging Tree: Execution and the English People 1770–1868* (Oxford: Oxford University Press, 1994).

Glasgow, Gordon, 'Clarke Aspinall: Liverpool Borough Coroner' *Lancashire History Quarterly*, vol.3, issue no.1, March 1999 and vol.3, issue no.2, June 1999.

Glasgow, Gordon, unpublished M.Phil. *The Work of Coroners*.

Graham, Anne E. and Emmas, C., *The Last Victim: The Extraordinary Life of Florence Maybrick, the wife of Jack the Ripper* (London: Headline, 1999).

Gosden, P.H.J.H., *The Friendly Societies in England 1815–1875* (Manchester: Manchester University Press, 1961).

Grey, Peter, *The Irish Famine* (London: Thames & Hudson, 1995).

Havard, J., *Cambridge Criminal Studies series 1862*.

Havard. J.D.J., *The Detection of Secret Homicide* (London: 1960).

Hammerton, A. James, *Cruelty and Companionship: Conflict in Nineteenth-century Married Life* (London: Routledge, 1992).

Hartman, Mary S., *Victorian Murderesses* paperback edn (London: Robson, 1977).

Heidensohn, Frances, *Women and Crime*, 2nd edn (London: Macmillan, 1996).

Heidensohn, Frances, 'Women and the Penal System', in *Women and Crime*, edited by A.Morris and L.Gelsthorpe (Cambridge: 1981).

Himmelfarb, Gertrude, *Victorian Minds* (London: Weidenfeld & Nicholson, 1952, 1968).

Hopkins, Eric, *Working-class Self-help in Nineteenth-century England* (London: 1995).

Kanya-Forstner, Martha, *The Politics of Survival: Irish women in outcast Liverpool, 1850–1890* (Liverpool University: Thesis Ph.D., 1997).

Knelman, Judith, *Twisting in the Wind: The Murderess and the English Press* (Toronto: University of Toronto Press, 1998).

Leonard, Eileen, *Women, Crime and Society* (New York and London: Longman, 1982).

Morris, Allison, *Women, Crime and Criminal Justice* (Oxford: Blackwell, 1987).

Norman, Philip, 'The Woman who Hanged for Love', *The Sunday Times Magazine*, 30 July 2000, pp. 16–23.

Nott-Bower, William, *Fifty-two Years a Policeman* (London: Edward Arnold, 1926).

O'Day, Rosemary, *The Family and Family Relationships 1500–1900* (London: Macmillan, 1994).

Pember Reeves, M. *Round About a Pound a Week* (London: Bell, 1913).

Roberts, Elizabeth, *A Woman's Place: An Oral History of Working-class Women: 1890–1940* (Oxford: Blackwell, 1984).

Ross, Ellen, 'Survival Networks: women's neighbourhood sharing in London before World War One', *History Workshop Journal*, 15 (1983).

Ross, Ellen, '"Not the sort that would sit on the doorstep": respectability in pre-World War One London neighbourhoods', *International Labour and Working Class History*, 27 (1985).

Rubenstein, William D., 'The Hunt for Jack the Ripper', *History Today* 50 (5) (2000), pp. 10–19.

Smart, Carol, *Women, Crime and Criminology: A Feminist Critique* (London: Routledge & Kegan Paul, 1976).

Tebbutt, '"You couldn't help but know": public and private space in the lives of working-class women, 1918–1939' *Manchester Region History Review* (1992).

Thompson, Paul, *The Voice of the Past: Oral History* (Oxford: Oxford University Press, 1978).

Vickery, Amanda, *The Gentleman's Daughter: Women's Lives in Georgian England* (London: Yale University Press, 1998).

Walvin, James, *Victorian Values* (London: Cardinal, 1988).

Whitford, William, 'Three cases of arsenical poisoning', *The Lancet*, 1 (1884), pp. 419–21.

Whittington-Egan, Richard, *Liverpool Colonnade* (Liverpool: Philip, Son & Nephew, 1955).

Wilson, Patrick, *Murderess: A Study of Women Executed in Britain Since 1843* (London: Michael Joseph, 1971).

Wohl, Anthony S. (ed.), *The Victorian Family: Structure and Stresses* (London: Croom Helm, 1978).

Zedner, Lucia, *Women, Crime and Custody in Victorian England*, paperback edn (Oxford: Oxford University Press, 1994).